AUTOSPORT *FILE*
Williams

AUTOSPORT FILE
Williams

TEMPLE PRESS

First published 1988 by
Temple Press
an imprint of
The Hamlyn Publishing Group Ltd
a division of
The Octopus Group PLC
Michelin House, 81 Fulham Road
London SW3 6RB
and distributed for them by
Octopus Distribution Services Ltd
Rushden, Northants NN10 9RZ

Produced by Bay View Books Ltd
Bideford, Devon EX39 2QE
Designed by Gerrard Lindley
Additional material from David Hodges
Picture research by Jeff Bloxham and Paul Harmer
Typeset by Lens Typesetting, Bideford
Reproduction by Isca Reprographics, Exeter

ISBN 0-600-55663-8

Printed by Mandarin Offset in Hong Kong

CONTENTS

Introduction

by Quentin Spurring

A new series of books, presented under the general heading *Autosport File:* here is a publishing 'natural'. Like the Formula 1 World Championship itself, our weekly *Autosport* was founded in 1950. Since then, we like to think, it has established itself as an effective voice amid the great (and growing) hubbub of motor racing worldwide.

Autosport, since its first, tentative issue 38 years ago, has grown with the sport, flourished with it: no doubt an increasing number of magazine-related projects will play their part in its further expansion as we pursue greater successes in the nineties.

The decision to involve the magazine in this new *Autosport File* series, then, was relatively easy. Choosing the Grand Prix teams with which to introduce the series, well, that was much more difficult.

It is a curious fact (and one speaking volumes about the nature of the business) that the Formula 1 teams that have achieved real, consistent success can be counted virtually on the fingers on one hand. The two teams with which we now present the *Autosport File* series are among this elite. They are Williams and, in the first companion volume, Lotus.

Williams Grand Prix Engineering, by the standards of most of its rivals, is a relative newcomer to the scene. This factor, actually, is responsible for much of the team's popularity, because Frank Williams started on the road to his very

Frank Williams, whose perseverance and determination produced, out of nothing, one of the world's foremost motor racing teams.

considerable success in Formula 1 within the clear memory of a majority of the current fans of Grand Prix racing. As his many supporters know very well, this remarkable man has produced out of nothing one of the world's foremost motor racing teams, and he has done so in the face of considerable adversity.

Perseverance has been the key to this exceptional success story. Frank Williams has inspired a great many people by revealing the full extent of what can be achieved when business acumen is allied with dogged determination.

Williams learned the Formula 1 ropes by fielding cars bought from established constructors before entering the fray with

his own car as recently as 1973. He waited until 1979 for his first victory, which was achieved, to his delight as a fervent patriot, in the British Grand Prix. That result opened the floodgates of success that shows no sign of being dammed: Williams scored four more wins that same season and has been one of the dominant constructors ever since, and never more so than in 1987. The tally already stands at 40 victories, placing the team fourth in the list of all-time winners, with many years fewer in the game than those above.

Prior to that extraordinary 1987 season, which produced a third World Champion for Williams and a fourth Constructors title, Frank Williams was partially paralysed by what would otherwise have been an innocuous road accident. It is a great tribute to him that he had equipped his team with such thorough professionalism that its performance was unaffected. This is typical of a man who formed a new Grand Prix team at a time when all around him said that he was foolish in trying to take on the establishment: in a few short years, Frank Williams has placed his team among the great ones of Formula 1.

The turbo cars took over in 1983. Williams was one of the last teams to make the inevitable switch, the Grand Prix of Europe at Brands Hatch marking the team's last race using the Cosworth DFV V8. Rosberg made his way up from a poor grid place to be sixth, until his engine broke at half distance.

right
Keke Rosberg and Nigel Mansell were excited by the prospect of their new FW10s fitted with the powerful Honda V6 turbo engines, a combination that eventually returned Williams to the forefront of Grand Prix racing.

below
For two seasons running the World Championship eluded Nigel Mansell.

Season by Season 1977-1987

by Nigel Roebuck

The Grand Prix editor's seasonal surveys have been a leading feature in a midwinter issue of *Autosport,* and these extracts trace the story of Frank Williams' team from 1977 when he regained his independence to the momentous 1987 season when his drivers won more than half the Grands Prix and Williams won the Constructors' Championship for the fourth time.

1977

Frank Williams, who was a free spirit once more after his brief partnership with Walter Wolf, also ran a March in 1977, for Patrick Neve. Anyone who witnessed the Belgian's one and only F2 drive, at Silverstone in March, would agree that his talent is considerable. A contemporary of Ribeiro, who drove a works March, Neve has usually proved conclusively quicker, but he found the car impossible. There was nothing at all wrong with the pre-

paration, for the Williams car's reliability record was highly impressive. But, when all is said an done, it was still a March 761, and all who drove one this year found the experience unpleasant.

1978

Alan Jones emerged as a real top-liner in 1978, as did the entire Williams team. It was a source of enormous pleasure to everyone that Frank, after years of paying last year's bills with this year's sponsorship money, finally had his head well above water. No one in Grand Prix racing has more guts and determination – or love of the sport, for that matter. With a gorgeous little car from Patrick Head's drawing board, substantial Arab backing and Jones in the cockpit, this was an utterly serious Formula 1 team. The jokes about Frank have long since stopped.

The team threatened to win a Grand Prix on more than one occasion. At Long

Although the car was not capable of real success, Patrick Neve helped re-establish Frank Williams as a team manager once again. The significant logo on this March 761 is Saudia on the rear wing.

*The neat Williams FW06
designed by Patrick
Head which, with driver
Alan Jones and huge
backing from Saudia
Airlines, was to pave the
way for future success.*

*An inspired drive by Alan
Jones was poorly
rewarded with only
seventh place at Long
Beach in 1978. The
Australian had fought up
to fifth and, despite a
sagging nosecone, was
holding on. Then a fuel
pressure problem
caused a misfire and
slowed him.*

above
At Monaco in 1978 Jones held a defiant sixth place in the early laps until an oil leak onto the rear brakes steadily grew worse and caused retirement.

left
Patrick Head's new FW07 for the 1979 season was not ready until the Spanish Grand Prix, where both Clay Regazzoni and Alan Jones showed distinct promise before retiring with engine failure and puncture respectively. But at Silverstone, the Williams dominated, Jones heading his team mate and the previously all-conquering Renaults until his engine blew up spectacularly.

Beach and Hockenheim, Alan was particularly outstanding, but the team's best result was a second place at the Glen. Reliability did not match competitiveness in 1978, but that would change.

1979

Patrick Head's new creation, the Saudia Williams FW07, made its debut in the Spanish at Jarama, and from the outset the chassis was sensational. It was also urgently needed. In the early races of the season, the FW06 was suddenly uncompetitive in a field of ground-effect cars. Only at Long Beach, where ultimate grip is relatively unimportant, had the ability of Alan Jones got the car into the reckoning.

FW07, however, was something else again. At Zolder, it was the fastest thing in the place, but broke; at Monaco, Jones was pushing the Ferraris, but clipped the wall; at Dijon he finished fourth on unsuitable tyres . . .

From then on, though, the Australian was almost impossible to stop. Silverstone

Clay Regazzoni about to secure Williams' long awaited first GP victory at Silverstone in 1979 following the demise of Alan Jones' FW07.

he utterly dominated before retirement, and after that came three Grand Prix wins on the trot: at Hockenheim, the Osterreichring and Zandvoort. At Monza, he was the fastest man in the race, albeit at the back after a stop; at Montreal he won superbly after a classic battle with Villeneuve; at the Glen, he took an easy pole and looked set for victory when a botched tyre change led to the loss of a wheel. Just like Andretti in 1977, Alan won more races than anyone else, yet finished only third in the points standings.

Attempting to rate Grand Prix drivers is an infinitely difficult task these days. By their own admission, the drivers' contribution is less now than it was five or ten years ago, simply because of the way the Formula 1 car has evolved. Today's driver is physically unable to compensate for shortcomings in his car – "With a ground-effect car, you have to drive on rails. You can't pitch it in sideways to try and get round its faults," one driver told me this year. "If you haven't got the basic grip there, you might as well go home." The proof of this pudding is easily found:

at Hockenheim this year, Clay Regazzoni qualified sixth and finished a fine second to his team mate, Jones; twelve months earlier, in the Shadow, Regga had failed to qualify!

So what does one say of Alan Jones in 1979? His approach to his job is much like Villeneuve's. When they arrive at a circuit, they are there to drive a racing car, pure and simple. All the peripheral aspects of the weekend – the politics, the posing and so on – leave them cold. They want no distractions from the job in hand. And it shows. Of course both would like to be World Champion, and they consider the most straightforward route is by winning all the races. It is no coincidence that they have provided most of the entertainment this year.

Jones' natural way with a racing car is to drive it as quickly as possible at all times. After many years of indifferent cars, it is a habit which he has found hard to break. Alan and a Shadow DN8 were good, flat out, for a place in the first 10; Alan and a Williams FW07, flat out, were good for the front. I find it inconceivable that he suddenly blossomed into a potential World Champion last winter. Simply, in 1979 he has had the right equipment, and the world notices only winners.

Patrick Head's new design set the standard. You had only to stand at the entry to Stowe during practice for the British Grand Prix to see it. Not only did the car turn in astonishingly well, it did so at a speed quite beyond the reach of any other. What should not be overlooked is

Regazzoni celebrates his British GP triumph flanked by second-placed René Arnoux, left, and third man Jean-Pierre Jarier. Although this was the Swiss driver's only GP success of '79, Jones went on to win the German, Austrian, Dutch and Canadian Grands Prix to end up third in the Drivers' Championship.

Carlos Reutemann's debut for Williams in the 1980 Argentine Grand Prix ended in retirement. Trying to pass Piquet's Brabham he was forced to take to the escape road, spun on to the grass and clogged the radiators. Alan Jones, meanwhile, had drawn clear to open his season in tremendous style.

that Jones was able to go with it all the way, at Silverstone and everywhere else. Over the years he has become a very considerable Grand Prix driver; only now does he have the car to be able to show it. Jones and Villeneuve must share the unofficial title of 'Driver of the Year'.

And then, of course, there was Gianclaudio – over the hill, finished, second-rate, winner of the British Grand Prix, who seemed to score points for Frank every fortnight. Putting down Clay Regazzoni's ability was a cottage industry in motor racing for years. Through the 1970s he achieved a very great deal, and his attitude to the job remained as pure as when he started out. Regazzoni was the most realistic of all Grand Prix drivers, precisely aware of his worth in all departments of the job. He was not a political animal, nor full of self-importance. There are those who drive Formula 1 cars better than he, none who enjoyed it more. There is nothing fragile about Clay's ego, which was why he was able to cope easily with being a number two driver. In a paddock increasingly full, it seemed, of sour expressions, it was always a relief to see Regazzoni's perennial bandit grin.

1980

Jones and the Williams team took it all in 1980 because they eliminated most of the factors which can bring failure. To get Alan to that title took on the proportions of a Holy Crusade for everyone in the team. And if their application to that task took its toll of their former lightheartedness, they could argue – with justification – that you don't win battles by having a good time. Up the ante, up the pressure.

The importance of 'the team' cannot be overstressed in the case of Frank's boys. Yes, they had all the ingredients – a superb and already proven motor car, constantly uprated and refined, first-rate mechanics, bountiful sponsorship, two of the world's best drivers – but they also had the right recipe, and that separated them from their rivals. At very few races this year was the car out-and-out quicker than any other. But while the competitiveness of Brabham, Ligier and Renault varied considerably, Williams were always there.

Patrick Head is a man not merely brilliant behind a drawing-board, but also

thoroughly practical at the circuits, able to rationalise problems calmly, then to solve them.

"One of the main things about Patrick," says Jones, "is that he designs a car very much with safety in mind. And that gives a fantastic amount of confidence to a driver." The proof of that was in Alan's every move. Like Stewart and the Matra MS80 or Peterson and the Lotus 72, Jones and the Williams FW07 were meant to be.

Different qualities take men to the World Championship. Look at the raw aggression which produced pole position at Zolder. Pironi's Ligier was quickest, and Alan had to abandon his car on the circuit when the engine cut. Arriving back at the pits, he found that Carlos Reutemann, his own engine blown up, was out in the one and only T-car. Time was ticking away. When Carlos stopped to hand over the car, Jones was about ready to get the pole on foot. As it was, he allowed the car to help him along, and the result was a remarkable lap right at the end of the session.

Then there was Jones the fighter, who never gave up his pursuit of the Ligiers at

Paul Ricard, or of Jabouille's Renault at Zeltweg and Hockenheim.

To my mind, however, his two most impressive drives came after mistakes. At Zandvoort, after tearing a skirt off while leading, his performance was quite sensational, the more so since there was nothing tangible to be gained by going so quickly. He was laps behind, yet drove to the limit – as in similar circumstances at Monza last year – because that is what comes naturally to him. At the Glen he goofed at the first corner and dropped to 12th. There were dollars at stake, but the championship was already clinched – ideal conditions for an uninhibited drive through the field. Which he gave us.

He did a lot of thinking, too, this demonstrated nowhere more effectively than at Monte Carlo, where he outgunned Reutemann away from the first chicane by the simple expedient of snicking down to first gear. Simple? Nobody else did it . . .

Then there is his remarkable stamina, an ability to set a daunting pace from the very start, and to sustain it for the rest of the race. All in all, he had a lot of cards to play.

As happens frequently to the man apparently heading for the title, the pressure began to get to him in the month of August, so that by the time Zandvoort came around he was, by his own admission, irritable and uptight. The Dutch Grand Prix weekend went all wrong for him. Piquet, his nearest challenger, won, as he also did a fortnight later at Imola. The momentum seemed to be slipping away from Alan, but in Canada all was well under control.

Both the Williams drivers enjoyed phenomenal reliability from their cars, particularly in the second half of the season. Seldom do results match aspirations, but the events of 1980 mirrored the ambitions of Frank Williams, outlined in a 1979 interview. Particularly impresssive was the team's reaction to losing those nine points at the Battle of Jarama. Certainly they felt sore about it – and still do – but rather than let bitterness intrude upon their endeavours, they simply buckled down to the task of winning the title *without* that win.

Whereas Alan Jones did everything we expected of him this season, Carlos Reutemann was something of a disappointment, yet it seems fatuous to say that of a man who finished third in the World Championship, who won the Monaco Grand Prix, and who took points from 11 out of 14 races. "I'm taking Carlos," said Williams, "because he's going to be the man who'll sit behind Alan all the way, and take over if something goes wrong." On most occasions, in this Reute-

Victories in France and Britain had sent Jones to the top of the championship – and made up for the disqualification from the Spanish race. At Zandvoort the Australian survived this crash at Hugenholtz during qualifying.

Jones displayed his fighting qualities at Zandvoort. On the opening lap he charged from row 2 around the outside of his team mate and the Renaults. However, it all went wrong at Hugenholtz, where he slid wide and ripped a skirt off, and a pit stop was necessary prior to continuing three laps down.

mann manifestly failed, and for reasons which are not apparent.

On six occasions Carlos outqualified Alan. That came as no surprise, for the Argentine has been one of the very quickest drivers for close to a decade. But in most of the races Jones quite simply left him behind, and on the odd occasion when something *did* go wrong for Alan, his team mate was usually too far back to take over. He did a perfect job at Monaco, and drove really magnificently in Spain where Jones was in trouble from the start. Eventually, of course, he was punted out of the race by Laffite, and we never saw quite the same vigour from him again. Quite possibly his ribs, battered in the accident, troubled him more than he cared to say.

Curiously, Reutemann very rarely looked like a winner in 1980. He was always in the reckoning, of course, but seemed to settle into a rhythm not quite on the pace. At Ricard he followed Arnoux's Renault endlessly, never once giving the impression that he would get by. At Brands he left too late his attempt to catch Piquet, and at Zandvoort became bogged down behind Andretti's Lotus 81.

The Dutch Grand Prix plainly highlighted the difference between the two Williams drivers. As Carlos struggled with Mario, Jones' sensational comeback drive brought him quickly up to them. There was no messing around from the Australian as he quickly dispensed with both of them, whereupon Reutemann suddenly came to life, passed the Lotus and put in a

lap faster than any of Alan's! And this was quite often the case, even when Jones finished way ahead.

When Carlos is inspired, his driving is a joy to behold. And his quick laps during practice at Monaco and Imola were quite beyond the scope of most Grand Prix drivers in deftness and flair. Which makes many of his lethargic race drives the more incomprehensible. His consistency in 1980 was unrivalled, but one was left with the thought that Clay Regazzoni, his predecessor, could have achieved almost as much. Members of the team occasionally allowed similar sentiments to surface.

1981

Jones did not retain his World Championship, but he should have done. It seemed to me that there was some extra ingredient in his driving this year: it was better than ever before. Any previous doubts of his inclusion among the great were expunged. No driver, of course, ever plays with the perfect hand, but Alan's remarkable combination of aggression, dash, stamina and opportunism made him unquestionably the best driver of the season. Competition is everything to him, what Patrick Head calls "pure animal instinct."

A.J. Foyt once said that, for him, racing was "just a matter of beating the other guys – not a romantic thing at all," and it is a philosophy to which Jones would subscribe. There are, if you think about it, many similarities between these two men. Both have a ready smile, explosive temper, excellent – if cruel – sense of humour, total awareness of their own standing, boundless self-confidence, and a passionate need to win.

I look back on this season and think of an Alan Jones who, despite being outqualified at 10 of the 15 Grands Prix by the numbing one-lap pace of team mate Carlos Reutemann, frequently towered over the Argentine at the flash of a green light. I think of him ducking past Carlos at Long Beach, capitalising on a mistake before you or I could blink, and I remember that chilling, vengeful pressure on Piquet at Monte Carlo, unflagging battles with Prost's faster Renault at Hockenheim and Zandvoort, leading the early laps at torrential Montreal.

Alan would have kept his title comfortably had not the fuel system problem,

which robbed him of victory in Monaco, recurred, unforgivably, at Hockenheim. By the same token, he would have been champion again had he not made a mistake while leading at Jarama. As always, he went out to win rather than not lose, and this very often costs dear. Las Vegas – which he loathed – brought a perfect performance. At my vantage point, the last corner, he was every lap a foot and a half nearer the inside wall than anyone else. And what is more, of course, he was doing that while travelling faster than they. All in all, it was probably the finest season by a defending World Champion since the days of Jimmy Clark.

As World Champion, Alan Jones began the 1981 season in great style, outmanouevring team-mate Reutemann to win the opening Grand Prix at Long Beach.

By July I found it almost inconceivable that Carlos Reutemann could lose the World Championship. Lean and superbly fit, Reutemann began the year in tremendous style – as he has always done. But this time there seemed to be a consistency missing from his nine previous Formula 1 seasons. He appeared to have a genuine belief that every race meant possible victory for him. His home Grand Prix, in Buenos Aires, drew perhaps the greatest drive of his career, and it was sad that his efforts could be so contemptuously swept aside by the hydraulically-suspended Brabham of Piquet.

top
Jones loathed Las Vegas but put in a brilliant drive.

Alan Jones, above, *and Carlos Reutemann,* below, *were both in contention for the 1981 World Championship. Their victories helped amass a total of 15 GP wins in three seasons for Patrick Head's FW07 chassis.*

Still, Nelson might call it justice. A fortnight before, in Brazil, Carlos had won. And, ironically, perhaps it was there that his World Championship began to slip away. In wet conditions he led from the start, tailed by Jones, and in the dying laps he decided not to observe the terms of his Williams contract – or the frantic reminders of it from his pit. He did not cede his position to Alan, for reasons which were readily understandable: a racing driver should always try to win.

Rightly or wrongly, however, he *had* signed that contract. Jones made no attempt to race with him, assuming that he would be waved by. Afterwards, the Australian was fit to be tied.

From that moment, Reutemann had a sure guarantee that his quest for the title would receive no assistance from his team mate.

For a while, it seemed that he might not need any. The points kept on coming, and he eased away to a huge lead. The victory in Belgium was particularly commendable, not for not any incredible feat of driving, but for the fact that he overcame private distress in a manner which I, for one, did not expect. Having, through no fault of his, run over a young mechanic in the pit lane, Carlos was distraught. But on race day he put aside his emotions, and got on with his job.

It all went wrong for Lole in the second half of the season: a blown engine at Hockenheim, a most uncharacteristic error of judgement at Zandvoort, a gamble on set-up at Monza. Nevertheless, he went to North America with a slender points lead, and his two drives there were among the most inexplicable I have seen. In Canada, his performance in the rain was, quite simply, pathetic – second to 19th in four laps.

And at Las Vegas, after scintillating form in practice, he faded to nothing in the race. Was he *really* in contention for the title, touching the hem of his life's ambition? It was hard to believe. Perhaps there *were* problems with his car, but that does not explain a total lack of aggression against a rival semi-comatose for the last quarter of the race, nor why a man on pole, with the World Championship beckoning, should have been fourth into the first corner.

It cannot be said that the commitment within the Williams team to get Reutemann that title was ever the equal of

the all-out support given to Jones the previous year. True, Carlos wanted for nothing in the mechanical sense, but the psychological push was never truly there.

Las Vegas, a pitiless place if ever there was one, was the scene of high tragedy in the life of a great racing driver. As Jones and Piquet took the plaudits. Reutemann slipped quietly away in his own private sorrow. How could it all have ended this way for a man of such colossal talent? Carlos' qualifying position at Monza was the result of the greatest single lap of 1981. Perhaps the simple truth is that he never relished a scrap. Perhaps he was never ruthless enough. Perhaps he dithered too much on last-minute tyre choice, and so on. Perhaps . . .

The title gone, Reutemann's sorrow at Las Vegas was all too obvious.

Keke Rosberg joined Williams for the 1982 season as number two to Carlos Reutemann. The Argentine, starting his 11th season of GP racing, drove brilliantly at Kyalami to split the powerful Renaults, and Rosberg earned two points with fifth place.

Friends or not, Jones and Reutemann easily brought another Constructors Cup to Williams, and you have to marvel at the way Frank and his men keep success from blunting ambition and eroding standards. Patrick Head's FW07 has now won 15 Grandes Epreuves in the last three seasons. Its success has come not through innovation – literally 'being a year ahead' – but from meticulous preparation, remarkable adaptability (at the hands of Patrick) and attention to detail. For all that, the fuel system pick-up problem, first apparent at Monte Carlo, took longer to solve than might have been expected – by which time it had cost both drivers points which would have kept the title out of Nelson Piquet's hands.

1982

In the high altitude of Kyalami the South African race was a turbo benefit, of course, but both of Frank Williams' cars finished in the points, and Keke Rosberg, fifth, started his campaign for the World Championship. It ended successfully at Las Vegas eight months later.

For years Rosberg had been hamstrung by his cars, although his talent and courage were never obscured. I remember practice at Brands Hatch in 1980, all that effort and fearlessness which none the less failed to get the Fittipaldi into the race. When Rosberg signed with Frank he had driven in 37 Grands Prix, and had precisely five World Championship points on his record.

The ways of the world are strange. If Alan Jones and Carlos Reutemann had not dithered over their futures at the back end of 1981, it is quite safe to say that Keke would never have been offered a Williams drive. Given reasonable notice of his stars' intentions, Frank would have signed Pironi or Piquet, but it was too late.

Rosberg, in the meantime, had made a decision. With nothing else firmly in view, he had nevertheless severed all ties with the Fittipaldi team, wisely figuring that there was simply no point in continuing like that. Better to be a free agent for a while and hope that something worthwhile would come up.

It did. For years Keke's talent and aggression and boundless self-confidence had been bottled up, and Frank's offer uncorked them. Rosberg was quick in a Williams from the first test on, and he was signed without delay. His early remarks about the legendary FW07 said a lot about the man: "How does it feel? Horrible, quite honestly, but all these solid cars feel like that. It's not much nicer to drive than the Fittipaldi. The difference is that when you try hard in this car you're up at the front of the grid instead of struggling to get onto the back . . ."

So there was no question of being overawed by joining the most successful team of recent years. Nor was he too concerned about the specification of the current cars. He liked them no more than anyone else, but in 1982 that was irrelevant. What mattered was that, for the first time, his car was competitive, an opportunity to be seized.

Over the entire season Rosberg did a better job than anyone else. Having watched his kerb-hopping over the years, I was not alone in wondering whether he would scupper himself by being *too* forceful, but these doubts were soon forgotten. Keke made only one mistake of consequence in a race (at Monte Carlo) and that, bearing in mind his intense competitiveness and the go-kart nature of the cars, was a considerable achievement.

It was always satisfying to see the World Championship – for all its overblown importance – go to an out-and-out racer, and Rosberg was certainly that. In 16 races his only 'percentage' drive was at Las Vegas, where the title was his for the taking and the Williams not ultra-competitive. That race apart, he always went for it.

People have said that Keke was not a true World Champion because he won only one race during the year, but that is surely nonsense. No driver had more than two victories in 1982, and none of his rivals, with the possible exception of René Arnoux, displayed Rosberg's race-for-race determination and commitment.

When a man leaves motor racing, there should be something more than mere statistics by which to remember and judge him.

Rosberg went to Williams as number two to Reutemann, who had decided finally to forget about retirement and accept Frank's very considerable financial inducement to return. Now, at last, Carlos was an unequivocal number one again, as he had been at Ferrari in 1978, his most successful season.

At Kyalami the Argentine was at his magnificent best, and finished second, between the Renaults. For a man beginning his eleventh season of Formula 1, however, the drivers' strike – and its attendant unpleasantness – was all very disagreeable, and the cars, which hardly lent themselves to the kind of artistry of which Reutemann was capable, were not to his taste. After an unsatisfactory race in Brazil he said he had no wish to continue, after all, and this time the decision was final. Jones, Andretti and Reutemann, three men central to Grand Prix racing for a very long time, were now gone within the space of a few weeks. Mario made a disappointing one-off appearance for Williams at Long Beach, but Frank needed to find a permanent replacement for Carlos, and finally chose Derek Daly.

In the space of a couple of months, therefore, Rosberg went from being unemployed to leader of the World Champion team, and this coincided with the introduction of a new car, the first from Williams in three years.

FW08 looked 'right' from the beginning, small, neat and agile. Almost immediately its testing times were startling. Before the car had been seen at a race Jonathan Palmer, for all his very limited experience, had shattered the Silverstone record with it.

And Rosberg, testing at a variety of tracks, was blindingly quick. Perhaps Nike Lauda was right: "The problem with the whole water tank thing was that Frank's new car was too quick too soon, and its times frightened people. If it had been maybe 20 kilos under the 580 limit, perhaps nothing would have been said, but it was much more than that . . ."

In fact, FW08 had been designed by Patrick Head to have a racing weight of around 540kg (the new legal minimum for 1983), and there were occasions during qualifying when it was considerably

*Jones and the FW07 –
a mighty combination –
waiting to practise
at Long Beach,
watched over by Patrick
Head.*

*Derek Daly heads Elio de
Angelis in 1982 at Zolder.*

Keke Rosberg battled on bravely against the turbo-powered opposition in the Cosworth-engined FW08 in 1983, Monaco providing the highlight (here at the exit from Casino Square).

Keke Rosberg tested the six-wheeler at Silverstone (pictured) and at Donington.

Rosberg, far side, and Laffite (who failed to qualify) retired from the 1983 Grand Prix of Europe at Brands Hatch, the last race for their Cosworth-powered FW08Cs (although Jonathan Palmer drove one in a one-off race for Williams in 1983).

Mario Andretti had a brief and disappointing drive for Williams at Long Beach, replacing Reutemann who had quit the team after the Brazilian GP.

Derek Daly was signed to partner Rosberg for the remainder of the '82 season, and the likeable Irishman ran well on several occasions. He finished fifth at Brands Hatch and nearly won at Monaco, at the end of the confused race when leading contenders ran out of fuel.

Keke Rosberg during qualifying for the 1982 British Grand Prix at Brands Hatch, where he took pole position.

left
Despite the shuffling of drivers, Williams remained competitive throughout the year. More and more time was devoted to seeking the optimum race day set up and perfect reliability, as here at Brands Hatch.

lighter than that. But the protest by Renault and Ferrari at Rio changed everything. FISA disqualified the cars of Piquet and Rosberg, which was a dumb thing to do, since nothing antagonises like retrospective punishment.

At the same time FISA 'clarified' the rules regarding the minimum weight limit, for that, Jean Sage and Marco Piccinini maintained, was the reason for their protest. If water tanks were kosher, then Renault and Ferrari would spend more millions in the quest for lightness. In future, said FISA, the cars would be weighed as they came in directly after the race. Nothing could be added in the way of coolants, fresh brake pads, etc. And that, contended the FOCA heavyweights, was a new rule and not clarification of an existing one. Routine topping up had always been allowed, a time-honoured custom, if not actually a rule. If nothing could be added before the weight check, then the limit was effectively being increased. On that basis they felt justified in giving Imola a miss, needing "more time to prepare cars to meet the new rules" (although Tyrrell managed it within a day or two). If the Rio results had been allowed

to stand, perhaps their reaction would have been less trenchant.

Whatever, Head and his colleagues had a new problem, that of making their car competitive in its new 'heavy' state. It took time. Although the FW08, in Rosberg's hands, led most of its maiden race, at Zolder, it was not an easy car to drive, its short wheelbase 'nervousness' making full demand on Keke's terrific reflexes - just as the Tyrrell 006 of a decade past needed a Jackie Stewart to get the best from it.

Underbody and skirt changes improved the car steadily through the season, and the Williams team began to devote more and more of the now farcical 'qualifying days' to seeking an optimum race day set-up. They played around with tyre pressures, sacrificing some early-race speed to have a car which came into its own as the afternoon wore on. Thus, Rosberg was in perfect shape in the closing laps at the Osterreichring and Dijon.

Frank also spent a lot on engines, in terms of development as well a quantity. "Don't get too upset," John Judd told a despondent Roberto Guerrero during practice at Dijon. "Apart from chassis dif-

ferences, remember that you're 40 horse-power down on Rosberg before you start . . ."

And of course, there was always the remarkable Williams reliability. Perhaps the team did win only once in 1982, whereas McLaren, for example, had four victories. The fact remains that their *overall* competitiveness was greater – they were never, unlike McLaren on occasions, flat off the pace, and their finishing record was bettered only by Ferrari, Rosberg won the World Championship, despite winning just once, and that says everything about his team's standard of preparation. He was nearly always there at the end, in the points on 10 occasions (excluding Rio), and could have taken the title without that Dijon victory.

Reutemann's retirement gave Derek Daly his big opportunity, and Williams personnel stress that he played a big part in the development of the FW08, but somehow the results never came together, and the open-faced Irishman was replaced by Jacques Laffite at season's end.

Sometimes Derek looked excellent. He convincingly led the non-turbo race in the opening laps at Paul Ricard, and had a very strong, if unrewarded, drive at Hockenheim. With the same tyre combination as Rosberg at Dijon he might well have been up there at the end. But in the races he rarely looked on a par with Keke,

and there are differing opinions as to whether he had the same equipment. Frank says yes, Derek no. All told, though, Daly did a far better job than eight points might suggest, and it is sad that he is out of work at present.

Before the start of the season Williams said that his great ambition was to win the Constructors' Cup for a third consecutive season, a feat never before achieved. In this he failed, and perhaps it is one of those hat tricks – like winning Indy – which is just not meant to be. The title this year went to Ferrari, for the tenth time, and the result was just. Consider the grief and turmoil at Maranello this year, that four different drivers scored points for them, that they won despite missing two races and running but a single car in six others, and the reliability and sheer pace of the 126C2 come sharply into perspective.

1983

The Williams team faced difficult times in 1983. Despite winning but a single race the previous year, their overall consistency and wonderful preparation – allied to Rosberg's formidable ability – had been enough to take Keke to the World Championship. Despite the Finn's hopes that the new regulations might actually close

After only eight weeks with the team Rosberg became number one driver. In Austria Rosberg was defeated by just .0125 seconds by Elio de Angelis (Lotus) after a mighty effort.

The 1983 World Championship will be remembered as the year of the pit stop. The teams' crews worked to a fine art to refuel and change all four tyres mid-race in a matter of seconds. Rosberg waits to rejoin the Detroit GP and take second place.

the gap between turbo and Cosworth, he and Frank knew in their hearts that this would be a season of frustration.

Towards the end of 1982, of course, Williams had been reminded fairly harshly of Formula 1's dog-eat-dog nature. Mansour Ojjeh's TAG company, one of Frank's major longtime sponsors, announced that it had taken over the financial end of the Porsche V6 turbo engine programme, commissioned by Ron Dennis of McLaren. Purely a commercial venture, asserted Ojjeh. Well, yes, but . . . the fact remained that a Williams sponsor was forking out for a turbo engine to benefit a rival team. All Frank could do was put a brave face on it, keep his private thoughts to himself.

Certainly, however, he was not about to stand in line behind Dennis for this 'TAG' engine, just as he had wisely come to the conclusion that there was no percentage in queueing behind Ecclestone for a BMW. Instead he worked away at Honda,

and the time was well spent. Kyalami showed us that.

The South African race, however, was the last of the year. For the previous 14 Rosberg and new team mate Jacques Laffite had to soldier away with the venerable DFV, now in its 17th year of Grand Prix competition. Patrick Head produced a very neat and tidy 'flat bottom' edition of the FW08, and put it on the pole, to a general chorus of amazement.

In 1983 terms, though, Rio was a freak race. Thereafter Rosberg usually had to be content with heading the Cosworths in practice and race, although on tight, acrobatic circuits the FW08C in his hands was always a serious factor. Until the mid-season break his results were stunning. After Montreal, indeed, he was only five points off the championship lead, and would actually have been in front without that absurd disqualification from second place in Brazil.

The second half of the year, though, was a different story. Once the championship trail hit the really fast circuits – Silverstone, Hockenheim, Zeltweg – Rosberg, Williams and Goodyear were no match for Lauda, McLaren and Michelin, let alone any of the serious turbos. At Spa Keke had been able to cling on to the hem of the turbo train, but later there was no question of that. These were races to be endured, an obligation to be met. Back at Didcot the Honda-powered FW09 was taking shape.

In the meantime, of course, the Japanese engine was actually in competition, for John Wickham's Spirit team made its Grand Prix debut at Silverstone. And we did begin to wonder if Williams had made the right choice, for Stefan Johansson's car was never without a misfire, and there did seem to be an awful lot of blow-ups. By contrast, though, Williams-Honda testing proved astonishingly

trouble-free from the first, which inevitably prompted doubts about engine installation design on the Spirit.

The FW09s appeared at Kyalami, and Rosberg rather shook everyone by qualifying sixth, and finishing fifth, far and away the most impressive 'turbo' debut by any team. After a relatively backwater season, Messrs. Williams, Head & Co served notice of intent for 1984.

One of this team's great strengths is continuity. Despite offers from pretty well everywhere – "Every single turbo engine was available to me for 1984" – Rosberg wisely took himself off the transfer market early in the game. By mid-August he and Frank had agreed terms for a third year together, and Laffite, despite undeniably disappointing form for much of the season, will indeed finish his two-year contract with the team. Although Williams and Laffite have always been good

On the really fast circuits, Rosberg, the Williams FW08 and Goodyear were no match for the turbo cars. At Silverstone Rosberg gets down to the business of qualifying.

right
Jonathan Palmer, here leading Raul Boesel's Ligier through Paddock Bend at Brands Hatch, had carried out much of the testing of the FW08 the previous year and was given a one-off race in the 1983 Grand Prix of Europe. He was the only Williams driver to finish and took a well-earned 13th place.

below
In the last race of the season, at Kyalami, the FW09s turned out, Rosberg qualifying sixth and Laffite, too, demonstrating that the new turbo car would suit him, although his race came to a premature end.

friends, Frank is not retaining Jacques out of sentiment (which would be quite simply unrealistic at today's prices), but because his faith in the Frenchman remains. And quite right, too.

In the weeks and months following Villeneuve's death, I formed the belief that Rosberg had inherited the mantle of the fastest in the business, and this season that conviction became more firmly entrenched. For me, the most exciting sight of 1983 was that of Keke pitching the Williams through the second righthand flick of Eau Rouge at Spa. There follows that long uphill drag where turbo muscle is everything, and only by exiting Eau Rouge miles an hour faster could Rosberg hope to stay in touch.

That was a miraculous drive (even if it yielded only fifth place), and came only seven days after Keke's memorable

triumph at Monte Carlo. The track was wet, and he took a gamble on tyres. From the way he disappeared in the early laps one might have believed that only he was on wets. In fact, only he – of the leading runners – was on *slicks*. It was a totally mesmeric blend of confidence and flair and courage that we saw that afternoon, and I doubt that any other driver of today could have produced it.

As we watched the sheer energy of Rosberg's efforts, week after week, it was hard to believe that this was not a man in the rudest of health. Keke is not a man to labour any problems, and spoke only rarely of his liver complaint. He did not feel ill, he said, merely listless. With his tyres falling apart he drove to the limit to win the unimportant Race of Champions, and that says it all about Keke.

Laffite began his second spell with

Although Rosberg's only 1983 win, at Monaco, was scored with a non-turbo car, he later proved that the new Honda TAG engined Williams was a match for the best. It was given an impressive debut in the South African Grand Prix which closed the season, Rosberg finishing fifth.

right
right
*Jacques Laffite made an
impressive return to
Williams in 1983, as
number two to Keke
Rosberg, and led briefly
at Long Beach; but it
seemed his driving style
was not that suited to the
FW08C and he often had
a hard time of it, here at
Brands Hatch for
instance.*

below
*An encouraging start to
the '84 season: from
ninth on the grid Rosberg
fought up to be second
to Alain Prost in the
Brazilian Grand Prix.*

Williams impressively, actually leading a
while at Long Beach until his Goodyears
gave up. As always he raced better than
he qualified (at Monza and Brands Hatch,
indeed, he missed the cut altogether), but
his curious and unique driving style –
early turn-in, tight line – did not suit the
FW08C. Jacques often had a hard time in
getting his tyres up to temperature, and
simply could not emulate Rosberg's
exuberant tail-out way of doing things. At
Brands he was plainly concerned, unable
for once to shrug off disappointment, but
at Kyalami his confidence was back. The
Honda-powered car was much more to his
taste, and he was quick once more.

1984

For the third year running, Williams won
but a single race. And, as in 1982 and '83,
this came primarily from the virtuosity of
Keke Rosberg. His brilliance at Dallas, the
most closely fought Grand Prix of the
season, was memorable. Like Villeneuve's famous victory in Spain, it was
against the run of play, a race which
should not have been won by that car.

Frank came late into the turbo game,
and always recognised that the first year
would be difficult. But I doubt that he and
his men were prepared quite for the problems which confronted them in 1984.
The Williams-Hondas had made their

left
A Honda engineer with Rosberg during practice at Imola. After starting from an encouraging second row position for the San Marino Grand Prix, Rosberg retired after only three laps with electrical problems.

below left
The packed engine bay of the FW09. The original Honda V6 turbo engine promised much in terms of raw power but was fragile.

below
Rosberg was somewhat fortunate to gain points for fourth place at Zolder behind the all conquering Ferrari of Michele Alboreto, the FW09 having run out of fuel.

debut in distinctly promising style at Kyalami, the final race of the previous season, Rosberg qualifying sixth and finishing fifth. By any standards that was encouraging, and when we went back to South Africa for round two this season Keke was beaten only by Piquet in practice.

The race, though, was a different matter. Rosberg led the opening lap, but the Williams looked as if on a skidpan, twitching and scrabbling to get its power down. It looked that way at the final race, too, as Keke again managed to lead the opening stages.

The FW09 always looked clumsy, the very last thing you would expect of a Williams, for Patrick Head's designs have always been paragons of nimbleness. For his first turbo car he opted again for a monocoque of aluminium/honeycomb, and in truth it seemed unable to cope with horsepower. Lightening work over the winter following its first race probably contributed significantly to the car's subsequent flexing problems.

The Honda V6, too, lacked rigidity, a serious failing in a modern Formula 1 engine, and its shortcomings did not end there. No one could doubt the sheer top end horsepower, but the engine's usable rev band was smaller by far than any of its rivals. The power came in with a wallop, and that served only to amplify the chassis deficiencies.

Drivers following the cars reported that they could always tell that the horsepower had finally arrived by the way the tail would abruptly kick sideways. On top of everything else, of course, Williams were on Goodyears in a season when you most definitely needed Michelins. These were very difficult cars to drive, the last device you would choose for a place like Dallas.

Rosberg's abiding complaint was the FW09's unwillingness to follow its front wheels. To set any sort of time, he said, you had to toss the car into the corner, then balance it all out with the throttle. All of which, as I mentioned earlier, made for pleasure if you were watching, mounting frustration if you were in the cockpit.

And Keke's frustration came through with increasing clarity as the year progressed. A man of his character does not care for supporting roles, and all through that final Cosworth season his impatience for a turbo was manifest. He wanted to get on terms again, but the Williams-Honda very rarely allowed him to do that.

He came away from Dallas with a victory, but was not fooled. If track conditions had been normal, the car would have been nowhere near Lotus and McLaren. But the rallycross surface made for an artificially slow pace – 10 seconds from qualifying times, remember – and Rosberg was always in touch. It was the others, in their surefooted cars, who made the mistakes. Keke, with his air-conditioned skull cap, kept a cool head. *He* won the Dallas Grand Prix, the car merely his transportation.

If Rosberg won only once, he reminded us constantly of his class. After an awful start at Zolder he was 20th on the opening lap, yet was up to second before half-distance. And what of Hockenheim? Sixteenth on lap one, fourth on lap nine! And out on lap 10 . . .

Final practice in Portugal, however, gave us the finest illustration of Keke's controlled aggression. With only a few minutes left, he was abandoning yet another blown up car out on the circuit, not yet even qualified. A lesser man would have panicked, run back to the pits and been in no fit state for a last ditch run in the T-car. But Rosberg took his time, judging the minutes to a nicety. Out he went . . . one inspired flying lap . . . fourth quickest.

Keke's irreverent sense of humour was probably the saving of him. As the season

wore on, anger was increasingly replaced by a kind of weary resignation.

Jacques Laffite was the perfect antidote to the team's serious-mindedness, usually managing to retain his grin through all tribulation. During the season there were occasional flashes of the old Laffite, days when he was scarcely slower than Rosberg, but usually the Frenchman was out of the main action. Among his staunchest allies was his team mate, who has always maintained that, in competitive cars, there would be precious little between them.

In the Williams-Honda, though, Jacques was pretty cautious. If it is cynical – and perhaps inaccurate – to deduce that, at 40, you don't put your balls on the line to qualify 15th rather than 18th, it is also reasonable. On occasion his perennial good humour was shattered by outbursts of genuine bitterness, and he would

claim, as did Derek Daly before him, that he was not getting the same equipment as Rosberg. Laffite did not leave quite as amicably as one might have expected.

He returned to Ligier, and Keke stayed on for the second half of his two-year contract. The great Finn's F1 career was rescued by Frank at the end of 1981, but it is a debt which he has more than paid off.

1985

Back from nowhere, in 1985, were Williams, and I was delighted. Since Alan Jones' retirement at the end of 1981, Frank's team had been pegged on a single victory a year, and each was primarily the consequence of Rosberg virtuosity. Williams made the turbo switch later than most, of course, this a temporary penalty

Jacques Laffite had a dreadful season in 1984, encountering several engine failures, but he occasionally showed his true skill.

for sensibly opting to tie themselves to a manufacturer working solely for *them*, rather than quickly joining a queue at Renault or BMW.

Patrick Head bristles a bit at criticism of his FW09, the first Williams-Honda, but the fact remains that the men who drove it – Rosberg and Laffite – had seldom a good word for it. Williams had a very poor season in 1984, partly through chassis deficiencies, partly because the original Honda F1 V6 – basically the old F2 motor with a blower – was fragile, and delivered its not inconsiderable power like an on/off switch.

In 1985, though, came FW10, Head's first carbon composite monocoque, and Rosberg was enthusiastic from the outset. At the opening race of the year, indeed, Keke and new team mate Nigel Mansell qualified second and fifth. For the first four races, though, they were stuck with

the old engine, and went to Canada with only four points on the board.

For reasons which have never been clear to me – beyond those of Oriental pride – we were led to believe that the engines for Montreal were "revised," although by the end of the season Williams personnel freely admitted they had been "all-new" – which, of course, everyone knew at the time: "It's lightly revised," grinned the mischievous Rosberg in Canada. "It's got six cylinders, hasn't it?"

However, ours not to reason why, etc. The difference in nearly all respects – power, torque, fuel efficiency, and, initially, reliability – was staggering, although throttle response was only marginally better. Despite two pits stops in Montreal, Keke finished fourth, driving absolutely flat out all the way. And a week later, in Detroit, he and the Williams-Honda faced no genuine challenge.

Poor reliability set in again, though, soon after mid-season. Engine-related problems put Rosberg out at Silverstone, Zeltweg, Zandvoort and Monza. In Belgium, however, both cars finished in the money, and thereafter the season was all Williams-Honda. At Brands Hatch the cars were in 'B' spec, with pull-rod rear suspension, new gearbox and lower rear bodywork, made possible by repositioning the electrics. Rumours persist that these changes were accompanied by yet more 'lightly revised' engine work. Be that as it may, the Williams FW10B has yet to lose a race.

I thought Keke drove better than ever in 1985, disappointing only during practice at Monaco, and his pole position lap at Silverstone stands, for me, as the great memory of the season. Earlier in that session, remember, he set a time with a slow puncture in the left front which was beyond anyone else!

Keke remains the great improvisor of Formula 1, the heavy smoker whose stamina seems yet unequalled. If freak conditions are likely, if a track surface is breaking up, if the hot is really torrid, the race unusually long, my money would always be on him.

He is always worth watching, with that lurid, darty style. Even on a straight, Rosberg's car looks nervous, as if its steering were two-fifths of a turn, lock to lock. His way of pitching a car into a corner, reminiscent of the ground-effect era,

New Williams signing Nigel Mansell and stalwart Keke Rosberg were most enthusiastic about Patrick Head's new FW10 even though both drivers had to start the '85 season with the old engines. Mansell opened his score with a fifth at Portugal and another at Imola, having been bundled out of the season opener in Brazil.

Rosberg's FW10 at Spa in 1985.

makes heavy demands of the Goodyear Tyre and Rubber Company, but who can deny that it works? Those last few laps at Kyalami were unforgettable.

Keke is simply a natural charger, and it is a remarkable fact that, despite all the vigour and flourish, he makes probably fewer mistakes over a season than any of his contemporaries. He is, however, not a man to cross on the race track, not one to forget a bad turn. At Brands Hatch he was incensed by Senna's blocking tactics in the early laps – and Ayrton paid for that.

At the top level, such tactics as Rosberg's need no justification. Less laudable was the brake test he gave Capelli in practice, after the Italian had unintentionally blocked him. A word in the novice's ear afterwards would have been preferable. In Adelaide Keke drove a perfect race, calmly in control while Senna fooled around behind him.

After too many fruitless seasons at Lotus, Mansell went to Williams and thrived. It can have done his morale no good over the years to see Lotus's frequent attempts to replace him, but at Williams he was given the impression from the first that he was there because they wanted him there. In an entirely positive atmosphere Mansell's pained expression disappeared, and his driving in 1985 was usually superb.

Life with Williams began badly for him, however. At the first corner of the first race, Rio, Nigel and Michele Alboreto laid claim to the same piece of tarmac at the same time. But by Monaco – a place he loves – Mansell was confident and swift enough to outqualify Rosberg, and he was to do it seven times more.

Qualifying, though, is one thing. Nigel has always been strong on the single blistering lap. During the second half of

At Brands Hatch Nigel Mansell fulfilled his earlier promise when he won the 1985 Grand Prix of Europe. Taking the lead on lap 9 he had a somewhat lonely but nonetheless demanding run to record his first GP victory.

the year his race performances were of the same quality, but not until Brands Hatch did he finally win a Grand Prix, at the 73rd time of asking. It was a cool and competent drive, victory the sweeter for being before a British crowd.

Kyalami, however, was a different matter. At Brands he had had a lonely afternoon, such pressure as there was coming from within himself, but in South Africa he produced a brilliant drive from pole position (and what a lap *that* was!), showing no sign of anxiety as he calmly held off Prost. It was that afternoon which showed us how far Mansell has travelled in a year. These were the only back-to-back victories of 1985.

To his courage and ability he has now added confidence. At Kyalami, from the beginning of practice, you somehow felt that he was expecting to win. He knew now it could be done. My chief memory of Nigel this year, however, is not of either of his wins, or the charge to second in Belgium, but of the final practice session at Silverstone.

The bare statistic is that he qualified fifth; the truth is that if that race had been other than the British Grand Prix, he might well have sat it out. Only a fortnight earlier he had been severely concussed in a massive shunt at Ricard, caused by tyre failure. To run at Silverstone at all was the decision of a brave man. To be within a couple of tenths of the front row was pure mind over matter, and prompted a word of tribute from Rosberg.

After a certain amount of controversy between them in 1984 many doubted the wisdom of Frank's decision to pair Keke and Nigel. But while it would be less than the truth to suggest they became friends this year, there was no evident animosity.

1986

Over the winter everything looked to be going the way of Williams. They had finished 1985 as very much the team on the rise, Mansell taking two of the last three races, Rosberg the other. Keke's

decision to go to McLaren had seemed like sense when he made it, at mid-season. Now, as he won his final race for Williams, you had to feel almost sorry for him.

Coming in was a further reduction in fuel capacity, from 220 to 195 litres, this FISA's latest 'safety' ploy to reduce speeds. Nonsense, the constructors quietly said, the cars will *still* be much quicker than in 1985. And, of course, they were right.

Honda did extraordinary work in preparing for the 195-litre limit, providing Williams with an unmatched power-to-consumption ratio. Thus, Mansell and new team mate Piquet found themselves with an advantage such as Prost and Lauda enjoyed at McLaren in 1984, when fuel limits were first introduced.

Brands put it most clearly into focus, the two Williams-Hondas vanishing into a race of their own, battling furiously the whole way, finishing more than a lap ahead of the third car – Prost's McLaren, which had run minimum boost all afternoon simply to be sure of going the 196 miles.

After that race Alain said he now saw the World Championship as a fight between Nigel and Nelson. With a demonstrably superior power:consumption ratio, he said, you can choose your advantage, tailor it to the circuit of the moment. You can run the same wing as the rest, and paralyse them in a straight line. Or, at a downforce track like Brands, you can run more wing, taking your advantage whenever the road turns. And, if the occasion demands, you can play with your boost switch in the reasonable certainty you have fuel enough to make the finish.

At Hockenheim, where Piquet won

Nigel Mansell won two of the last three races of '85, then crashed out on the opening lap at Brazil in 1986, while Piquet went on to win. Mansell thought he had won in Spain, but Senna, following here earlier in the race, pipped him in an incredible 'photo-finish'.

Keke Rosberg, pictured
at Monaco, had a
frustrating 1984 season
in the FW09.

below left
Nigel Mansell in 1985,
the year he 'came good'.

below right
Piquet and Mansell
hammer past a McLaren
at Imola in 1986.

Waiting to go out to the grid for the 1985 Grand Prix of Europe, Mansell, far side, and Piquet line up in the pit lane. Mansell was to score his first GP victory in this race.

At times Piquet was something of a enigma: at Monaco in 1986, for instance, he never really got into the race.

The real quality of the team Frank Williams had built up showed in Rio – just three weeks after his dreadful accident returning from Paul Ricard testing. Nelson Piquet waves his national flag after clinching the opening round of the 1986 World Championship.

with almost laughable ease, the two McLarens – on minimum boost all the way – ran dry on the last lap. Nelson pulled into the scrutineering area and proceeded to rev his engine hard for a few seconds before shutting it down. No fuel problems there.

It was by no means all Honda, though. Patrick Head's FW11, an evolutionary design derived from the FW10, was slightly longer than its predessor, but very much lower – especially at the rear, which allowed a cleaner air flow onto the wing.

FW11 never looked a wayward car, and nor was it. Mansell, uniquely able to compare it directly with FW10, raved about it from the beginning.

Consider, then, what Williams had going as the new season approached: a superb chassis, the best engine in the business, a very tidy budget, Goodyear tyres, two front-running drivers. In a journalists' poll, conducted in January, the vast majority – myself, alas, included – chose Piquet as the likely World Champion of 1986.

Then, on holiday before the season began, I met American Editor Gordon Kirby for lunch, learned of Frank's dreadful accident, unreported in the New York papers. There were but three weeks to the first race, and the real quality of everything Frank had built up at Williams Grand Prix Engineering beamed out in Rio, where Piquet emphatically won.

As Nelson and Nigel raced on to further successes, Frank bravely joked that the team seemed to function better without him. As his condition improved, strength began to return, he was able to play an increasingly active role, but his absence from the pit lane was perhaps more crucial than has been acknowledged.

By the end of the season Williams-Honda had 141 points in the Constructors' championship, only three short of a record. This was a title clinched long before Adelaide, yet Piquet would say, a few hours after the final race, that only the constructors paid any heed to that: what mattered was the World Championship for *drivers*. And that Williams somehow lost.

Soichiro Honda, present at a Grand Prix for the first time in 20 years, had two chances in three of watching his engine push a man to the title, yet had to smile inscrutably, shake the hand of Alain Prost.

There are pitfalls in running a genuine two-car team – and by that I mean one with a pair of number one drivers. Back in 1973 Peterson and Fittipaldi swept Team Lotus to the Constructors' Cup, but could not keep the genius of Stewart from the World Championship. Jones and Reutemann – the other pair of Williams drivers who never got along – did the same five years ago, but the title that mattered was nicked by Piquet at the last race.

For an equal two-car team to function at its best, you need discipline and integrity from everyone involved, as Prost, Lauda and McLaren International demonstrated to perfection for two seasons. Team orders were superfluous in that context because both drivers were mature individuals, able to reason that pooling their information would work to their mutual advantage.

So, there we were at the start of the season, all tipping Nelson for the 1986 World Championship. I based my forecast on a conviction that the Williams-Honda FW11 was going to be the best car, and a belief that Piquet – with Prost and Senna

Nigel Mansell holds aloft the Labatt Trophy, celebrating his second GP win of the 1986 season in Canada.

committed elsewhere – would be the best driver to get his hands on that car.

Thrown into the calculation, too, was the thought that Nelson, frustrated after a couple of virtually wasted seasons at Brabham, would be like a man reborn, keen to show the world that only poor equipment had kept him from the limelight in the recent past. And Rio, a straightforward victory if ever there was one, seemed to prove us smugly right.

Although Mansell had won twice at the end of 1985, there can be no doubt that Piquet came to Williams in the belief that he would sweep the uncomplicated Englishman aside, swiftly assert himself as undisputed number one. Winning in Rio – where Nigel crashed during the first minute – served to reinforce his confidence.

As well as that, Nelson had won at home, had beaten Senna, Brazil's new hero. In his own mind, he was Back.

But that was rather too complacent. Seven years at Brabham had left Piquet a little spoiled. There he never had a team mate capable of hustling him – nor a yardstick for his own performances. Everyone had doted on him, smiled indulgently at his schoolboy behaviour. He had been sheltered, in other words, from the realities of a world beyond Brabham. He didn't care for PR work, and so he didn't do it.

"In seven years with Parmalat," Bernie Ecclestone said, "the only time he spoke to them was fifteen conversations in three days when we were thinking of Senna for the second car . . ."

For all that, it began to bother Piquet that Prost was earning so much more, and through 1985 he decided he needed a sizeable rise. Bernie, gambling that Nelson was too comfortable at Brabham to make a move, declined to accommodate him. In a car park at the Osterreichring, therefore, Piquet signed his name to a Williams contract, in exchange for $63,461 a week, plus another ten grand per point. 'Poor old Nelson – if only he had a McLaren or Williams' . . . there would be no more of that.

Perhaps winning in Brazil worked against him, strange as that may sound, for he was anything but distinguished, with one or two exceptions, through the next seven races. True, he drove beautifully at Spa and should have won, but at Montreal and Ricard he was lacklustre at best, and in Detroit simply dropped it. And quite why he even bothered to get out of bed for the Monaco Grand Prix remains a mystery.

While Piquet flagged, Mansell thrived, even he a little stunned at the way victories were coming. Nigel, unlike Nelson, was doing justice to the best car in the business. And interested parties were beginning to ask why they were paying all this gelt for a superstar when the other fellow was winning all the races. After Ricard Nigel had three on the board, and Rio seemed like a long time ago.

At Brands Hatch Nelson looked more like the Piquet of old, taking a comfortable pole position. But in the race Nigel squarely beat him, and the Brazilian petulantly declined to shake his hand afterwards.

After his tyre change Mansell came out just in front of Piquet, who had stopped a couple of laps earlier. Nelson, understandingly hellbent on getting past before Nigel was up to speed, went for the inside at Surtees – and found the door quite legitimately shut in his face. *Any* Grand Prix drivers worth the name would have done that – including Piquet – but afterwards Nelson raged about it. When he passed Mansell for the lead at Monza, he flicked the wheel, forcing his team mate out wide, afterwards claiming that as retribution for the wrong done him at Brands.

Through the second half of the Williams season, it seemed often that here were two teams which happened to operate out of the same pit. Briefing – in the McLaren sense of the word – ceased to be.

After Brands Piquet came on strong, winning conclusively at Hockenheim and then, two weeks later, at the Hungaroring. Here, of course, Nelson – with the benefit of a T-car – tried a different diff during practice, found it markedly improved the traction and 'driveability' of the Williams on the slick surface, and used it in the race, having somehow forgotten to tell Nigel about it.

That did a lot for team spirit.

At Monza Piquet, outpaced by Mansell during qualifying, took a 'flyer' for the

Mansell takes the chequered flag at Paul Ricard, where his third GP success of the year put him at the top of the World Championship on level points with Alain Prost.

race, opted for a wing setting which had not been tried in practice – and it worked. During the closing laps he passed Nigel to win the race, and on the slowing down lap the Englishman drew alongside him and applauded!

"Were you congratulating him?" I asked. "Or were you doing the very last thing he would expect ...?" Mansell, himself becoming adept at the psyching game, just grinned.

That was the second Williams-Honda 1-2 of the season. Prost had scored nothing that day, and his earlier forecast – that Mansell and Piquet alone would dispute the title – looked to be coming true. After Estoril, where Nigel simply flattened everyone, it seemed as good as settled – but in Mexico everything went awry. Mansell's first gear did not engage properly, and he was left at the start. And Piquet, who led the first half of the race, threw away another bundle of points by

making riotous use of his tyres. He needed four sets for that race, where Prost made do with two. Alain, nursing a sick car, was allowed to finish second, and those six points – like the half-dozen scored in Portugal, spun away by Piquet – meant that the World Champion was still in the game when they headed off to Australia.

The tyre explosion on Mansell's car in Adelaide will remain – together with Diego Maradona's volleyball goal against England in the World Cup – as *the* sporting image of 1986. Cruising easily towards the World Championship became, in that brutal split-second, fighting for survival. For nearly a quarter of a minute we watched Nigel wrestle that car down to a halt, saw the left rear wheel twitch as the engine finally died.

Useless to say, now, that it was rotten luck and all that sort of thing. It was more than that. Mansell had won more races than anyone, and only one, in Belgium,

With minutes to go in the final qualifying session at Brands Hatch for the British Grand Prix, Mansell studies the computer screen to learn exactly what he must do. Although Piquet claimed pole position, Mansell left the pits after a tyre change just in front of his team mate, stuck to his guns and scored another hard-won victory.

Mansell led at Monza but Piquet, with a new wing setting, closed up to win, seemingly with no trouble.

had come with a measure of luck. Needing only to finish third in Australia, he had driven precisely the race required.

Afterwards team personnel said they had been on the point of calling him in for tyres, this immediately after learning of Rosberg's similar problem.

You will recall that Prost, having punctured a tyre, had come in for a new set after 32 of the 80 laps (and that, in any case, he had been intending to change at the halfway point). When Alain came back out, in fourth place, he was more than 20 seconds adrift of the Williams pair, yet quickly began carving pieces out of their lead. As his new tyres were obviously making so much difference, why, I wondered, did Williams not bring Mansell and Piquet in at that point? By the time of the tyre explosion, Nigel had already been passed by Alain, and Nelson was on the hook.

So, it was all gone, Wiliams-Honda won more than half the races, yet finished the year without a World Champion, and one was left with the thought that, against Alain Prost, you simply cannot afford any mistakes. Mansell and Piquet had at their

disposal the fastest car in the business, and one of amazing reliability. Preparation was superb, as ever, and Williams tyre stops were consistently the best in the business – far better, for example, than those of McLaren.

When Prost won at Hockenheim in the T-car two years ago, having switched immediately before the start, we cited that as an example of real quality in a team. At the British Grand Prix Mansell did the same. In all matters technical, it was difficult to find fault with Williams in 1986.

But the situation which arose between the drivers should not have been tolerated by the team management. Piquet kept quiet about the trick diff in Budapest, and won the race. Had he retired for any reason, the victory would have gone, not to his team mate's Williams, but to Senna's Lotus.

You could feel nothing but intense sympathy for Mansell at Adelaide. Piquet outqualified him in eight of the 16 Grands Prix, but in the races Nigel was solidly the better of the two. Nelson, in my opinion, would not have been a worthy World Champion in 1986.

Had Piquet, in the words of one team manager, been "found out" since his move to Williams? Had he never been quite the ace we all imagined? Or had he simply got lazy, and found that moving to a new team, with an absolutely competitive team mate, was a shock to his system? When Frank signed Nelson, he described him as "the best driver in the world," but that he most assuredly was not in 1986. Simply, there were too many mistakes.

Mansell, by contrast, continued to surprise us. For many years I was one of the legion who believed Nigel very quick, very brave, but not a man to become a regular Grand Prix winner. It pleases me that we were wrong. The victories at Montreal, Ricard and Brands were from the top drawer, but for me the highlight of his season was that amazing drive in Portugal. He had seen his championship lead whittled down, and the psychological momentum move Piquet's way. There were three races left, three other men who wanted the title, and he just drove away from them. In 1986 Mansell did himself – and his team – proud.

1987

At Rio, it was fine to see Frank back 'on duty' in the Williams pit, and his drivers made him very happy during qualifying. One-two they were, in the 1:26 bracket, with Senna next up, on 1:28.4. Prost was three full seconds away, the Ferraris more than four. If this was how it was going to be, the 1987 Grand Prix season was already a yawn.

After all this time, we should have known better than that. Race day was a different matter. Alain and McLaren topped the warm-up times, calmly strolled away with race while the Williams-Hondas boiled in the heat.

Through 1986 – Frank's convalescent time – the animosity between Mansell and Piquet had mushroomed. The Williams team has experienced similar difficulties in times past. Even now, mention of Reutemann causes Jones' lip to curl; and Alan assuredly likes Carlos more than Carlos likes Alan.

So 'personality clashes' between his drivers are nothing new to Frank. It would be different, he said, in 1987 when he was back on the scene to keep an eye on

things. He would stand no nonsense. Drivers, after all, were only employees.

Frank's sense of optimism has always been one of his highest cards. It has never faltered; but on occasion it has been misplaced, and this was one such. The Mansell/Piquet relationship, apparently rock bottom in '86, found a way to go downhill in '87. And, within the team, it seemed that all were powerless to influence it.

Through the summer, to the distress of some readers, I was critical of Piquet, whom I consider a lazy race driver, often using only a sliver of his talent. You can argue far into the night, if you wish, that the Brazilian's natural gift is greater than Mansell's: beyond doubt is that a hundred per cent of Nigel's ability is worth more than ninety of Nelson's – and much of the time that is what Williams Grand Prix Engineering has been getting these two years past.

Either that, or Piquet was spectacularly overrated in his Brabham days. You can't have it both ways.

So what has changed in the last couple of seasons? What has changed is that, for the first time since 1979, Nelson has been teamed with a partner who constitutes an accurate barometer of his own performances. Thirty-odd races he and Mansell have done together, and nearly always he has come off second best – on pace, if not points. Too often he has blamed the barometer. *Mea culpa* is not his way – nor Nigel's, for that matter.

A case in point: during the last few minutes of the British Grand Prix, as Mansell closed him down, Piquet ran his fastest laps of the race – yet afterwards claimed that he could do nothing about his team mate, that his tyres had gone to hell in the late stages.

It looked straightforward to me: Nelson had fallen for the oldest trick in the book, been sold a dummy, jinked left when Nigel jinked left, then left the door into Stowe wide open.

After defeats at Mansell's hand, Piquet has mumbled *ad nauseam* about his team mate's dangerous tactics. He has also complained repeatedly about his treatment from the team, who did not, he maintained, fully acknowledge or respect his status as number one driver.

Perhaps he should have jogged their memories by driving faster than the supposed number two. Or as fast, anyway. If Williams began to regard Mansell as their

At Rio at the start of the 1987 season Piquet, watched by Frank Dernie, was actually speaking to his 'rival team mate' Nigel Mansell, even if it was by way of the radio line and not face to face.

Nigel Mansell dominated from pole position at Monaco until a broken exhaust halted his charge and presented victory to Ayrton Senna's 'active-suspension' Lotus-Honda.

star turn, it was hardly surprising: he was doing their winning for them.

Nelson won three races this year: at Hockenheim he inherited the lead when Prost broke with five laps to go; at the Hungaroring he moved into first when Mansell's wheelnut departed with six left; at Monza – Piquet's most out-and-out competitive race of the year – Senna's leading Lotus went off at Parabolica when seven laps from the flag.

So am I saying that Piquet is not a worthy World Champion? It matters really not. Quite often the World Championship brings nothing for the racers. It registers with me when the man who wins it is clearly the best of his time. Thirty years ago the same story was true. "You couldn't really take it seriously," Tony Brooks says, "any year that Stirling didn't win it. And Stirling *never* won it . . ."

After watching all 16 races, I shall look back on 1987 as a year in which Prost again showed himself to be the best, in which Mansell won the most races, and in which Piquet won the title. In that order.

At his World Championship press conference in Japan. Nelson spoke of his accident at Imola, and its aftereffects. He had been unable, he said, to sleep properly for much of the season since, added that his competitive instincts had been blunted, that he had driven part of the time "for points."

It was a dreadful shunt, which concussed him seriously and ruled him out of the race: no surprise to learn that it had taken its toll for some time afterward. It went some way towards explaining many of his lacklustre performances this year – but how could it account for his similar showings in 1986? For this season was in many ways a mirror of last. Undeniably Mansell outpaced him, and oftentimes Piquet looked anything but the ace we know he can be.

His fans will see it otherwise. They will point to his three titles, his charmingly plausible gypsy public manner, his always impressive performances before them in the British Grand Prix.

It won't do. As a consistent accumulator of points, he is superb, and a lot of people consider this an admirable way of going racing, if hardly in the stirring tradition of Peterson or Villeneuve. But as a World Champion, Nelson is seriously flawed: too many mistakes – and often too little use of his abilities.

Find me one of his fellows who would disagree. Find me one who rejoiced for him when the title was clinched. And don't hold your breath while you're looking.

I think we tired of Williams this season, in part because their superiority made for many a dreary race. In part, too, because the moaning got wearisome. We had Piquet complaining that Williams were giving preferential treatment to Mansell; Nigel suggesting that Honda's best was going to Nelson.

"For Christ's sake," another driver exploded in Mexico, "They win all the bloody races, and yet all they can do is whinge! It really must be awful to think you might only finish second . . ."

He had a point. The whole thing was getting terribly precious.

What does one say of Mansell, so near – so far – from the World Championship for the second year running. Six wins, twice as many as anyone else, but no title.

Prost had a lot of sympathy for him, recalling that twice he, too, missed the title by a whisker – despite *seven* victories in 1984. But Alain reduces the job of Grand Prix driver to its dimensions, whereas Nigel seems sometimes to magnify its difficulties. Prost seeks always to play down a problem, and this is the major difference between him and Mansell. He would never have got involved in that fracas with Senna at Spa, and I speak not of the accident (these things happen), but of the scenes afterwards.

And yet Nigel can make the winning of a Grand Prix look like the most straightforward exercise on earth. He can lead all the way, or he can pass the man in front with an incisive daring and commitment that leave you breathless. His moves on Piquet at Ricard, Silverstone and Zeltweg were each unforgettable.

In my opinion, Mansell drove even better this year than last. He won half a dozen of his 14 races, and should have had a least a couple more. He started eight times from the pole, the rest from second. These are statistics remarkable by any standards.

Going into the last two races, he trailed his team mate on points, yet many felt – despite Honda's preference for a Piquet World Championship – that he would do it at the last, just as Hunt did in 1976. Commitment would do the job. But it was all wiped away with a simple mistake, when

a brush with the kerb became a spin, which became an accident.

In the last two races, then, Williams failed to score a single point, missed their opportunity of setting a new Constructors record, and that was sad. Patrick Head's FW11B, with Honda power, was a magnificent racing machine, strong in every department.

Who really knows why the Japanese decided to split, to end such a successful partnership a year ahead of time? Was it that they didn't care to see Williams allowing Mansell to beat Piquet? The black mark incurred when the team refused to take Nakajima? Whatever, Formula 1 learned a lesson in 1987: before you get involved with Honda, be very sure to read the small print. And, having done that, get them to explain *precisely* what they mean by it. Don't imagine for a second they're in this thing for sport. Or, God Forbid, fun. We're talking commerce, where Formula 1 amounts to a speck in a Grand Plan.

This is not to suggest naivety on the part of Frank, Patrick or anyone else: probably they saw their job as winning races with, and for, Honda, and they could scarcely have done it to better effect. Probably they didn't kowtow to the degree required.

Still, there is a silver lining. They may have lost Honda's horsepower, but they have also lost Honda's Mr. Sakurai, the company's F1 Managing Director, by contrast with whom Arthur Scargill is personable.

Frank Williams and His Team

by Alan Henry

To understand the way in which Frank Williams operates his team, it is necessary to understand that Frank came up the hard way. And, although the pressures of doing Formula 1 business in the 1980s may well require him to dovetail his role as a team boss with that of a businessman, Frank is above all else a racer. Motor racing, being involved with his cars and attending the races are his number one priority. The rest of it is a means to an end.

When you visit the superbly planned, spacious and well-equipped factory on the outskirts of Didcot, it's as well to remember Frank's background. Frank started at the very bottom and, as he clawed his way up the rungs of the racing ladder, he was on the receiving end of a few kicks which sent him crashing back to earth again. When that happened, he picked himself up, dusted himself down and put his foot on the bottom rung yet again for another try . . .

It's a long time since Frank shared a notorious motor racing flat in Harrow with others of his ilk. A quarter of a century ago Williams had nothing to his name, apart from an unquenchable determination to get a toehold in the motor racing business. A penniless sometime saloon car racer, he slept outside the famous flat in the back of a van while such luminaries as Charlie Crichton-Stuart (later to work for Frank) and 'Bubbles' Horsley (Lord Hesketh's

Frank Williams soon began to gain a shrewd feel for sponsorship, and by 1980 had proudly added the name of Leyland to the other sponsors of his cars.

*Frank Williams with Piers
Courage in an
immaculately prepared
Brabham.*

future F1 team manager in the halcyon
days of James Hunt) slept like normal
mortals indoors!

To say that Frank was less than
successful behind the wheel of a racing
car is to understate the case. He was a
pretty poor performer and, although he
graduated to Formula 3, trailing round
Europe scratching a living, he never
achieved any worthwhile results. In truth,
he first made a serious motor racing
reputation when he began selling second
hand single seater racing cars in the mid-
1960s. From there it was a short step to the
role of entrant/team manager, a task he
has relished ever since.

Frank's company began preparing cars
for several private owners, but it was with

brewery heir Piers Courage that the sleek
dark blue livery of 'Frank Williams Racing
Cars' began to become a name in the
European Formula 2 Championship.
Frank was a stickler, demanding the
highest-standards of turn-out, and Piers'
Formula 2 Brabhams were amongst the
most immaculate cars racing in 1968. It
would have been easy, perhaps, for Frank
to have stayed in the second division, but
Piers had already had a taste of Formula 1
during his erratic in/out career with BRM.
He needed to reassert his own F1
reputation – and Frank wanted to move
up into the big league. So, in 1969, they
got their hands on an ex-works Formula 1
Brabham and tackled a World
Championship season.

Pleasing a sponsor: Williams with a 'boxed' Politoys car in 1971.

Piers made terrific progress and the Williams Brabham was as immaculately prepared as its Formula 2 predecessor. It was a great year, Piers barnstorming Frank's Dunlop-shod Brabham to second places at Monaco and Watkins Glen, defeating the Goodyear-tyred works car of Jack Brabham himself in the latter event, much to the ill-concealed rage of the Australian ace. And behind it all was Frank, directing things with a methodical, unflappable calm. He was getting good at his job.

Being overwhelmingly ambitious, Frank wasn't satisfied with merely running a second-hand 'off the shelf' Grand Prix car. What he wanted was a purpose-built racer exclusively for his team and he found a willing partner in Alessandro de Tomaso, the Italian constructor who had already gained experience building F2 and F3 machinery. Frank sank an enormous amount of money into the project and Piers stayed on the team strength to drive this new challenger.

Williams and his small outfit had high hopes for Piers and the new car, but the partnership was brutally torn asunder during the Dutch Grand Prix at Zandvoort when the car crashed at high speed and Courage perished in the ensuing fire. Apart from the fact that he had lost one of his closest friends the accident was a financial body blow from which Frank took years to recover. But, as history relates, recover he did.

In 1971, he was back fielding a March driven by Henri Pescarolo, a partnership which continued into the following year when Frank produced what was in fact the first Williams, although dubbed the 'Politoys' after the Italian model car maker who was picking up the tabs for its sponsorship. Then in 1973 he landed Marlboro backing in conjunction with the Iso Rivolta specialist car company, fielding his cars under the 'Iso Marlboro' banner. Sadly, despite the occasional flashes of promise, they were not successful and Frank entered a bleak period when his team was operating on

Nanni Galli and Howden Ganley in the Iso Marlboro cars.

Michel Leclere in the FW05 backed by oil magnate Walter Wolf fends off Alan Jones in a Lotus at Paul Ricard.

(and sometimes over) a financial knife edge. Finally only the intervention of Austro-Canadian oil magnate Walter Wolf saved the team from going bust. Wolf bought control of the team and, for 1976, Frank Williams Racing Cars suddenly turned into Walter Wolf Racing.

Frank was defiantly upbeat about the takeover at the time. "The team has changed in name only; everybody in the business knows that this is really Frank's team operating under another title," he bubbled at the time. But Frank was being an optimist and, secretly, he knew it. To put it bluntly, he became the highest-paid 'gopher' in the business. When he was forced to miss a Grand Prix because Walter wanted him to collect his new Mercedes-Benz from the factory, he knew that time had run out. A Racer couldn't handle that sort of situation.

By the end of the year Williams was on the move again, laying the groundwork for his World Championship challenge in 1980. With sponsorship brought by Belgian driver Patrick Neve, Frank acquired a new 'customer' March 771 and set up in a small way in time for the 1977 European season. It was a modest effort, but he was back in the business as a race team owner in the true sense of the word. And he had brought with him from Wolf the young engineer who had been assistant to Walter's chief designer Harvey Postlethwaite. The engineer's name was Patrick Head and the two men have worked together ever since.

In those early years, Frank's real forte was finding sponsorship. His determination and patience knew no bounds. The rebuffs and disappointments which are an inevitable part of such a process just bounced off him. He would chisel away until he had done the deal. And over the winter of 1977/78 he opened up the contacts which would guarantee his team financial stability for the next five years. He made contact with the Saudis.

Perhaps that is where Frank's shrewd 'feel' for sponsorship negotiations showed itself to best advantage. His first contact was with Saudia, the national airline of the Kingdom of Saudi Arabia, and once Frank had established the right connections, backing from Albilad (the trading company of the Saudi Royal Family) and the high technology Franco-Saudi company Techniques d'Avant Garde (TAG) followed. It is a measure of Frank's determination to clinch some of these deals that, at one point, he arrived at the London hotel of one of his potential sponsor's and asked the gentleman concerned if he would mind stepping out of the front door for a moment. At the kerb was a racing car on a trailer – painted in the proposed livery of the potential sponsor! It was a master stroke which served to clinch the deal on the spot.

The selection of Alan Jones as the team's driver for 1978 was also a turning point of considerable significance as the Williams team now had a man in the cockpit quite capable of running with the best of the opposition. Frank was immensely excited about Alan's potential from day one, and their partnership was to endure through to the end of 1981 when Jones decided, prematurely as things turned out, to quit the cockpit and return home.

Once the Williams team tasted success in 1979/80, it grew quite rapidly, just as the whole operational complexity of Formula 1 changed quite dramatically in

the early 1980s. With the turbo revolution getting into top gear, Grand Prix teams became appreciably less self-reliant as an increasing number of them became closely involved with major car manufacturers for their engine supply contracts. It was typical of Frank's independent streak – and his loyalty to the Formula One Constructors' Association cause – that the team was late onto the turbo bandwagon.

Patrick Head looks unconcerned as Jones waits to practise in South Africa in 1980.

The FOCA/FISA wars which almost tore Formula 1 apart in 1981 saw the Williams team management firmly drawn up on the FOCA side. In a nutshell, Frank was one of the most passionate believers in the FOCA cause – that's to say he officially supported the viewpoint that the refilling of brake cooling reservoirs in order to bring cars back up to the required minimum weight limit at post-race scrutineering was a thoroughly legitimate loophole in the regulations as they were written at the time. FISA's decision to plug this loophole by issuing a "rule clarification" sparked a succession of public rows and even the boycott by FOCA teams, including Williams, of the 1982 San Marino Grand Prix at Imola.

The over-zealous determination with which the by-now elitist Williams team management fought to promote the FOCA line suggested to some that Frank was a little too close to the wood to be able to see the trees. It was not a happy time for many people in Formula 1, and some people believe that the rift which opened up between the British press and Williams over that matter still slightly mars those relationships seven years afterwards.

When it came to selecting a turbocharged engine, Frank stuck out for the best deal he could find. He had no intention of standing in a queue behind any of his fellow team principals to do business with a major manufacturer – which is one of the reasons why nothing ever came of his proposed partnership with BMW, even though mock-up engines got as far as the factory in order that the business of installation could be examined and assessed.

In the event, Honda came aboard for the last race of the 1983 season, and a partnership which would endure through until the end of 1987 was forged. Shortly afterwards, in January 1984, Williams moved into its current purpose-built headquarters at Basil Hill Road, Didcot, having outgrown the hitherto piecemeal programme of expansion within a couple factories a mile or so away towards the town centre.

With Honda setting up its Formula 1 engine base at the Williams factory and the company expanding to take on additional staff of its own, it did not take long for the Williams payroll to expand to include over 100 people. At the end of 1987 a total staff of 112 was employed.

Although Frank remained the man in charge, retaining a majority shareholding in the company to this day, Patrick Head's loyalty, commitment and success were rewarded with a stake in the company in 1981. Moreover, the demands on the business administration side of the company were growing at such a pace by the end of 1984 that further rationalisation of its management structure was needed, so when Commercial Manager Sheridan Thynne was made a director in May 1985, it gave him added status and influence when negotiating with multi-national sponsors on behalf of Williams Grand Prix Engineering. Thus, by the end of 1985, Frank's company was quite well structured, with Patrick Head and aerodynamicist Frank Dernie looking after the technical side of the operation, and Sheridan keeping tabs on the commercial side in conjunction with the firm's exclusive sponsorship consultants CSS Promotions, who had played a major part in securing the lucrative backing from Canon which the team has enjoyed since the start of 1985. (Thynne left at the end of 1987.)

Frank had always been the motive power and inspiration behind everybody's efforts at Didcot, but the value of his strong management team was underlined dramatically at the start of 1986. Returning to Nice airport after the FW11's final pre-season Paul Ricard test session, Frank was involved in a serious car accident. He sustained spinal injuries which have left him paralysed and confined to a wheelchair, but in those initial, crucial few weeks immediately after the accident, his situation was so serious that there was a chance he might not even survive. But his management team simply took up the reins, operating the company with superb efficiency throughout the 1986 championship season.

It took most of the year for Frank's condition to stabilise to the point where he could even consider returning to work on anything approaching a serious basis, but once he was on the road towards rehabilitation he returned to his desk. He was absolutely determined to be back in business, at the pit wall, for 1987, and faithfully attended every race, including the punishing 'long haul' Mexico/Japan/Australia sequence at the end of the year, returning to England in the fortnight separating each of these events. "My home is better equipped to deal with me that any hotels," he says by way of explanation.

It is clearly more difficult for Frank to play as meaningful a part in the minute-by-minute operation of his cars in an F1 pit lane than it was before his accident, but those close to him are totally convinced that his enthusiasm for his team and cars provided the stimulus which led to his recovery. Make no mistake, Frank absolutely *lives* for motor racing, although he is happy to leave the commercial side to his lieutenants. "Frank is into tyres, drivers and the nitty gritty of the team's logistics," explains one of his close colleagues, "Preparing brochures for new sponsorship proposals is not really his scene!"

Frank is candid about where he fits into his own company structure in these high technology times. "Obviously my circumstances mean that it's not possible for me to fulfill quite the same role with the team at the circuits as I did prior to my accident," he explains, "and the onset of the current high technology means that the task of actually running a car has become a more complex and specialist business which has to be left to the engineers. The days of somebody like me controlling the team from the pit wall with a lap board and stop watch are long gone.

"But I don't mind this, I've simply adapted to changing times. I think I've become rather used to adapting to change over the last year or two. Who knows, in a few years there may be another shift of emphasis which may require us all to change the way we operate the team again, and in a different way. But it's no big problem. We adapt as we go."

As far as formulating company policy is concerned, Frank has the final say, "But I consult with Patrick on most things, obviously if they have anything to do with engineering, and with Sheridan perhaps if it touches on commercial matters."

Keeping sponsors and suppliers well disposed to the company is also a matter of prime importance. "I would like to think that our relationships with them are good to excellent," says Frank firmly, "although I don't have a lot of day-to-day contact with the suppliers. But we work hard at this side of the business.

"As far as our links with sponsors are concerned, apart from the more obvious

collaboration at individual races, we make the factory available for their people to look round from time to time, and give them the chance of entertaining important clients or senior executives here as well. We also encourage considerable use of our show cars. At the moment we have a couple of them, both FW11Bs to '87 specification, and we will probably have to use them throughout 1988 because I can't really see us having any spare FW12s available for that purpose much before the end of next season."

Talking about company strategy, Frank is adamant that he and his colleagues took

A characteristic shot of Frank Williams looking for one of his cars from a pit wall in 1981.

Piers Courage in typical extravagant style, practising at Silverstone.

Howden Ganley was among the drivers to appear in the eye-catching Iso Marlboro Williams in 1973.

Once Alan Jones had retired from the lead, Clay Regazzoni drove hard to record the first Grand Prix success for Williams in the 1979 British Grand Prix at Silverstone.

Francois Migault in a Williams FW04, which featured a Hesketh-type nosecone.

Misfortune hampered Alan Jones at Monaco in 1978. He was holding down a worthy sixth place when an oil leak developed, coating the rear brakes, which soon became less than adequate for the tight street circuit. But, as the season unfolded, Jones and Patrick Head's new FW06 made a strong impression.

Patrick Head, left, and Nigel Mansell worry over a Honda engine.

the correct course of action in dealing with Honda. While some people on the outside regarded it as an example of how not to deal with a major motor manufacturer, he thinks of it in terms of protecting the independence of Williams.

"Yes, in essence, that's the way we saw it, because I think it was clear that Honda was only really interested in finding a home for Nakajima as far as we were concerned. What came through quite clearly, from a number of remarks they let slip over a long period of time, was that they were absolutely intent on getting Senna in at McLaren. They had that in mind way back, from the winter of 1986/87. And there was no way in the world that we were going to play second string to McLaren – particularly as the Honda deal was our deal in the first place!"

Touchline observers tend to think that had Frank been in action throughout 1986 he might just have been able to influence

events to take a slightly different direction. He personally enjoyed a good face-to-face relationship with the Managing Director of Honda's Formula 1 programme, Yoshitoshi Sakurai, and got on well with other key figures within the Japanese company. In that connection it might be fair to comment that the Williams team lost even more than was immediately apparent from the hospitalisation of its boss throughout that crucial season. Patrick Head had his hands more than full tending the cars which won nine of the year's 16 races, so there was no spare time for him to turn his hand to major administrative matters of this nature. Japanese companies tend to like dealing with the top man when they do business with other concerns, so Frank's absence from the scene might inadvertently have rendered Williams GP Engineering unusually vulnerable to behind-the-scenes politicking.

Long-term, however, Frank does not believe that the team's prospects have been compromised. "It would have been far tidier to have continued our programme with Honda through until the end of 1988," he concedes, "and it has meant that we were obliged to initiate an interim programme with the Judd 3.5-litre engine while we get our bearings again. It may well be that we will carry on with the Judd engine for quite a while to come – or perhaps it might not be. It is something we will have to reassess once the 1988 programme gets under way."

The Williams team's commitment to race car engineering is total, but with the technology it has to hand there is always the possibility that the team could find an outlet for it in some sort of partnership with a major manufacturer. Some years ago Patrick Head drew on his specialist resources to help British Leyland with the development of a Metro rally prototype. A development of this nature could conceivably happen again, but Frank is cautious about allowing the company to diversify in this manner.

"As a general proposition, such partnerships look very attractive to us," he explains, "but when you get down to specifics, it is not really so straight-forward. I am anxious that we should not compromise our number one priority, which is racing. Agreed we have a range of certain specialist engineering skills, and both Patrick and I are convinced that somewhere there is an application for those skills to assist other concerns that don't have them and need them.

"Our business is winning motor races, keep that in mind. We could do deals tomorrow with this or that motor manufacturer. It may put cash in the bank, but it could cost us our winning capability. And that's not what we're here for."

Williams could be accused of being over-zealous about guarding his team's independence, of demonstrating a

Williams poses with Keke Rosberg's FW07 and an array of Leyland models before the team's successful 1982 campaign.

right
Frank, helped by his wife, was a guest of honour at the annual Doghouse Club Ball in November '87, when a cheque for £10,000 was handed over to Stoke Mandeville Hospital.

below
An emotionally charged moment: Virginia Williams, Frank's wife, accepts the Shell Oils British Grand Prix Trophy.

commercial inflexibility which will not prove beneficial in the long-term. Frank smiles indulgently at such suggestions. Needless to say, he doesn't accept such criticism as valid, pointing out that "Patrick is always accusing me of being too flexible on many occasions!"

Whatever the future may hold for this self-made man and his racing team, whether it be collaboration with a major car maker on a Formula 1 engine programme, or reverting to the route whereby his team's engines are supplied by a specialist race engine manufacturer, such as Cosworth or John Judd, the fortunes of the man who gives his surname to the team will be inextricably entwined with the organisation he has founded.

Frank Williams is an up-front boss and it's hard to see him ever relinquishing that role, pulling back and delegating more than he does at present. He wrote his own epitaph in an interview some 16 years ago, when he was struggling to run Pescarolo's Politoys March. It remains equally valid to this day:

"The secret of the success or failure of this team is me . . . "

Patrick Head on Formula 1 Design

by Doug Nye

Patrick Head and Frank Williams first met in the palatial lounge of London's Carlton Tower Hotel in November 1975. Frank had been hunting desperately for a new team engineer at the close of his most fraught Formula 1 season. Walter Wolf was in the wings, interested in buying control of the Frank Williams (Racing Cars) team, but with promises of alternative sponsorship for 1976 Frank still hoped to retain his fiercely prized independence.

Patrick had just been recommended to him as a talented and properly-qualified engineer with valuable racing experience. He had done some work for Formula 5000 owner-driver Guy Edwards, and it was Guy and Ian Phillips – then editor of *Autosport* – who had jointly suggested his name to Frank.

When they met, Patrick recalls how extremely smartly Frank was dressed, while he himself felt rather scruffy in such plush surroundings; "As we talked he gave not the slightest impression of being at all interested in me as an engineer – it was as though he'd talked with hundreds of engineers already and was weary of the whole thing. What he did ask was whether or not I was really committed. 'Are you prepared to work twelve hours a day, seven days a week?' he asked. And I said, 'No, I'm not, because anybody who has to do that is extremely badly organised . . . ' I'm not sure that Frank

Patrick Head (right) in discussion with Frank Dernie. Each has been a vital member of the successful Williams organisation.

Straightforward front suspension of Head's first Williams, the FW06, a simple, lightweight and effective design.

thought that was the right answer, but in any case I got the job . . ."

He was to spend twelve hours a day, seven days a week, working at it . . .

The story of how Walter Wolf then bought into the team, how Patrick found himself as assistant to ex-Hesketh designer Harvey Postlethwaite, trying to develop the 1976 Wolf-Williams FW05 – née Hesketh 308D – cars, is familiar. For 1977 Frank severed his Wolf ties and with Patrick as his chief – and only – engineer he set up Williams Grand Prix Engineering Ltd. They ran a basically two-year old March that first season for the Belgian driver Patrick Neve, then for 1978 Patrick designed the Williams-Cosworth FW06 car in which Alan Jones shone as "the best of the rest" outside Lotus and Ferrari that season.

In 1979 Patrick's FW07 ground-effects design made its debut and with five World Championship race wins WGPE became a Formula 1 force to be reckoned with. They won back-to-back F1 Constructors' Championship titles in 1980-81, and carried Alan Jones to the Drivers' title in 1980 and Keke Rosberg to it in 1982. With Honda turbo power in recent years, WGPE has again secured back-to-back Constructors' Cup titles in 1986-87, won the lion's share of the qualifying races and enabled Nelson Piquet to win his third Drivers' Championship title.

Looking back over his career thus far, Patrick Head – at 41 – is typically matter of fact. He will explain how he never dreamed of building a career in motor racing. His late father, Colonel Michael Head, had been a career officer in the

FLY saudia

above
FW07 laid bare, with the slim monocoque and the broad side pods of the ground effects era clearly shown.

top left
FW07, first ground-effects Williams, which in various configurations served the team so well.

left
Clay Regazzoni speeds on to record Williams' first ever Grand Prix victory at Silverstone in 1979, the FW07's fifth race.

Army, "Not a square-bashing soldier – more on the technical side, going up to the War office each day, committee stuff – he normally wore a suit rather than his Army uniform . . ."

But in his spare time he raced a C-Type Jaguar, then a Cooper-Jaguar sports car, and similar enthusiasm was soaked up by his son. Patrick was educated at Wellington College, coincidentally at the same time as both James Hunt and Peter Wright – true father of the ground-effects F1 car and of Lotus active suspension – though he knew neither at the time. A Naval career then almost claimed him, but after three months at the RNC Dartmouth he bought himself out. After a somewhat chequered further education

including periods at Birmingham University, Bournemouth Technical College, on a London University external course, and finally two years at University College, London, he "emerged as a proper engineer".

In 1970 he went to work for Lola Cars at Huntingdon where " . . . I found myself producing bits for everything from Formula Ford and Super Vee to Indianapolis and CanAm, 2-litre sports cars, 3-litre sports cars, Formula 5000 – just about every conceivable class of competition car. So rather than having just one top suspension link to draw you would find yourself being asked to draw twenty, all different, and you would discover very rapidly what not to do . . ."

PATRICK HEAD ON FORMULA 1 DESIGN

At Lola, Patrick worked alongside John Barnard, who had started there about a year earlier and who would leave some three months after him. They would subsequently become friendly rivals in Formula 1 design, Patrick at Williams, Barnard at McLaren and, in 1987-88, Ferrari.

Patrick left Lola, set up his own Super Vee engine preparation project, and worked with Michael Cane in designing and building a one-off F2 car for Aberdonian driver Richard Scott. Much of his investment in FSV engines was lost when a batch of them were melted in a workshop fire. Scott shunted the F2 car, lost interest and the project died. But he introduced Patrick to former Brabham designer Ron Tauranac, for whom he then went to work on Trojan F5000 and later Formula 1 projects in 1973-74. Building his own boat in the Surrey Docks seemed of greater interest through much of 1974-75.

"By that time I had to some extent given up any great motor racing ambition. I didn't look upon motor racing as a career as such. Up to a point it had just seemed a bit of fun, and then sailing seemed potentially better fun, and I kind of tripped from one bit of fun to another. I never really planned my future or looked too far in advance. I had virtually decided that racing was a mug's game and was comfortable with giving it up, when Frank happened to call and asked me to meet him. I wish I could say it was more structured, but it wasn't. I've never really seen motor racing as a proper job at all . . . It just didn't happen that way, not in my case."

Since he had already had his Formula 1 baptism with Tauranac's Trojan in 1974, helping in its design and build before attending four GPs with the team, his sudden induction into Williams did not seem a huge step.

"First entering Formula 1 engineering is far more of a step nowadays. Any young engineer joining a Formula 1 team today will find the whole approach vastly more sophisticated than it was in '75, much more in line with aircraft standards of engineering than those applied to any other kind of racing car." Patrick had worked with Ron – a legendarily hard taskmaster – for about eight months. He found it an illuminating experience, building upon that already gained at Lola Cars, but very different. "I learned tenacity, and a different way of producing cars.

Ron's approach was much more hands-on, almost sorting things out on the shop floor, whereas at Lola it was almost frowned upon if you, as a design draughtsman, ever dared leave the drawing office. Your language was the sheet of paper and that sheet of paper was your communication with the shop floor. If you had drawn the parts properly anybody, anywhere in the world, should be able to make them for you, and you should then be able to bring all those parts together in another part of the world and have a different group of people put them together properly – all from the drawings alone.

"The drawing is the language of the engineer.

"That's the way it really should be done, but Ron – partly through his high degree of impatience – always wanted it to happen in minutes, and he had this slightly more hands-on approach. People on the shop floor tended to get interested in the design process, interesting for them but it can give you grey hairs as well!"

So what are the pre-requisites for his kind of job?

"You've got to be a fairly determined character, otherwise you won't get very far in motor racing at all. Racing continuously deals out some pretty heavy knocks. If you care to spend much time sitting on your backside saying 'life isn't fair' then you're not going to get far in it. I think enthusiasm and determination are major requirements."

When he joined Frank Williams (Racing Cars) he found " . . . a pretty small set up, running cars which were sound but not especially advanced constructionally, so it really was just a small step up the ladder from what I had already been playing around with. In 1974 Frank had run a decent middle-ranking team, but in 1975 they had taken a bit of a dump and Frank was rushing around being the team manager and team engineer combined and everything was fairly run down when I joined . . .

"But you must remember that the rate of development in Formula 1 then was very slow indeed. Some constructional techniques were more advanced on Lola sports cars in 1970 than on Formula 1 in 1974 . . .

"The main question facing F1 engineers at that time seemed to be, 'What are these funny wings? What do they do? How do they work?' They had the biggest

The FW08 was a tidied-up and stiffened version of the FW07, with new front suspension. The tub was in aluminium as against the fashionable carbon/Kevlar.

effect on cars at that time, but nobody really understood them and I certainly include myself in that."

Through the awful Wolf-Williams season of 1976 Patrick effectively lay low in the trenches watching the shot and shell flying overhead at more senior targets. "I learned a lot about what not to do in Formula 1. We all made a welter of huge errors that year, which compressed several normal seasons' experience into one intensive period. I know the experience saved me from repeating some of those errors in later years. But it's not really profitable to dwell too much upon that season. There have been many bad Formula 1 cars, and the FW05 was just one of them. It was a bad, bad car, and it's best forgotten . . . "

One major lesson learned was to resist any temptation to make 'a quick bodge' in the vague hope it might improve the car. Occasionally such a stab in the dark might work well. But once it was built into the

car whatever else was done would only compound the bodge, and bodges are heavy – and compound-bodges heavier still. Into the 1980s, the Williams design ethic became broadly: "Try to do things once properly, rather than four or five times quickly and badly". Combined with the Frank Williams personal ethic of 'Excellence is not quite good enough', it was a formidably demanding but productive philosophy.

Once set free to design his own cars his own way from 1978, Patrick admitted to spending more time thinking what he wanted to do or to produce – thinking whether it was necessary or not and, if so, then exploring the very best method of production – before ever beginning a serious design drawing.

Not that one man really designs a Williams F1 car any more, as Patrick readily points out. "The media like to stick a label on a car and say it's designed by Patrick Head or by John Barnard or by Gérard

Ducarouge or whoever. That's simplistic. It's far too complex a process these days for any one man to claim exclusive credit. Our cars are a product of the Williams engineering department and I am fortunate in having some very good people working with me, each of whom can contribute greatly to the finished product."

Even when he set about designing his first Williams car – the FW06 – in the Autumn of 1977, he was not alone, although that project was actually assistant-engineer Neil Oatley's first experience of motor racing design.

"All of these cars with the engine doubling as part of the chassis are pretty modular in concept. Despite the need for compatibility of suspension and things you can really treat the back end independently of the front end as a basic design exercise. I think I worked round the rear suspension first, and then in those days the monocoques were conventionally folded-up sheets of aluminium, rivetted along the seams.

"The Lotus 78 had run well that season, showing the way towards ground-effect aerodynamics. I was reasonably aware it had gone quite well but not, I considered, *that* well. I hadn't really twigged what it was trying to achieve, although I should have done because John Barnard had talked to me about the Indy cars he was working on which were running with an enormous degree of rake in them – running steeply nose down/tail high made them very much quicker.

"So I designed an undertray for the '06 car, which looked at in retrospect would have made it very much faster. It was carried under the engine and extended right to the tail with an upswept diffuser shape formed into it. I had thought why raise the back of the car when one could more elegantly make its underfloor rise up from the back of the monocoque?

"We actually made a flat undertray, but the mechanics cursed it because it hampered quick engine changes, and I never followed up with the Mark II which would have been the shaped undertray with the diffuser bits on it. '06 was a perfectly sound conventional car but was terribly unreliable in 1978, which resulted from a combination of its fundamental design and of the way we ran it.

"My front hub assembly/wheel bearing for that car gave us a problem a couple of times . . . But we learned a great deal and

were able to follow up with the '07 which worked very much better once adequately developed . . . "

Patrick has often been branded a 'conservative' in design terms – his cars too often being regarded as fine developments of the best innovations made by other perhaps more daring designers. He seems unconcerned, comfortable with what one might deem an aspersion, but he will mildly point out the WGPE have never regarded self-publicity as an important part of racing, preferring their results to speak for themselves.

"You might also say that occasionally we have 'cheated' along with the best of them, by which I mean we have interpreted the rules as liberally as we felt we could get away with . . .

"But when it comes to basic design philosophy this company has one source of income – the sponsorship it receives from concerns who want the product exposure available from having their names on our racing cars. They don't sponsor us so that I can explore extreme ideas, and I am always conscious of that.

"Having said that, at times extreme ideas might bring us good results on-circuit, but I'm always aware that we've got to be out on those same sircuits somewhere at or near the front. We are not an adjunct to some enormous industrial group, and so we have no buffer to see us through a possibly extended bad period brought about by us exploring extreme ideas which don't deliver. When Colin Chapman was still alive, his reputation was such that even when Team Lotus had been through some terribly bad times there was always the expectation they were suddenly going to turn the corner by coming up with something new. And all the time the rest of the Lotus Group was somehow generating funds to keep the company afloat. Ferrari similarly have had some terribly low times, but the production car plant was always generating revenue to ensure survival.

"We have never had that buffer, and certainly in 1984 when we had our bad year with the FW09 and the early Honda engines, I felt the financial wind most distinctly . . .

"Some of our regular sponsors were extremely good in that period in terms of having confidence and faith that we could bounce back. But I feel it's very important for this company to do a consistently

Development of the six-wheeler reached an advanced stage. It is seen during tests at Silverstone.

sound job, and if you go for extremes – while it can sometimes pay off – if it doesn't you could be in real trouble. Once you have fallen off the tightrope in Formula 1, it's not at all easy to climb back on."

What really confounds the facile label of 'conservatism' where Patrick Head is concerned is such projects as the four-wheel drive Williams six-wheeler which "... would have been undoubtedly the only way for everybody to go had the rules remained stable. Certainly even now we'd be looking at four-wheel drive if Formula 1 permitted it, which it does not any longer. Wheel drag is a very large percentage of the vehicle's overall drag, and anything we could do to reduce that would be of great benefit. We were well prepared with the six-wheeler, not quite at the stage where we would have been happy with it as a GP car, but all our data from the wind-tunnel and track-testing showed conclusively that it was going to do the job.

"Similarly, active suspension. A lot of people have been talking of doing it, Lotus have a programme which they are pursuing strongly for commercial returns in the road car field, but in terms of race cars right now [the end of 1987] there are only two companies with active ride and they are Lotus and Williams.

"Their system is probably more adaptable than ours, but we have not yet seen any effect as a result of the system we have chosen to use which we would regard as being detrimental."

During 1987 it was also interesting to take a look at the rival cars which followed WGPE's lead in various areas of design.

The Williams FW11-series engine installation was effectively copied by both Lotus and Ferrari in terms of cooling systems, turbos, and inlet log configuration. The 1987 Ferrari also mimicked Williams's general gearbox layout, as well as the moulded-composite chassis and general car configuration. Ferrari in fact was able to improve upon the Didcot product, employing a lower engine and gearbox to advantage.

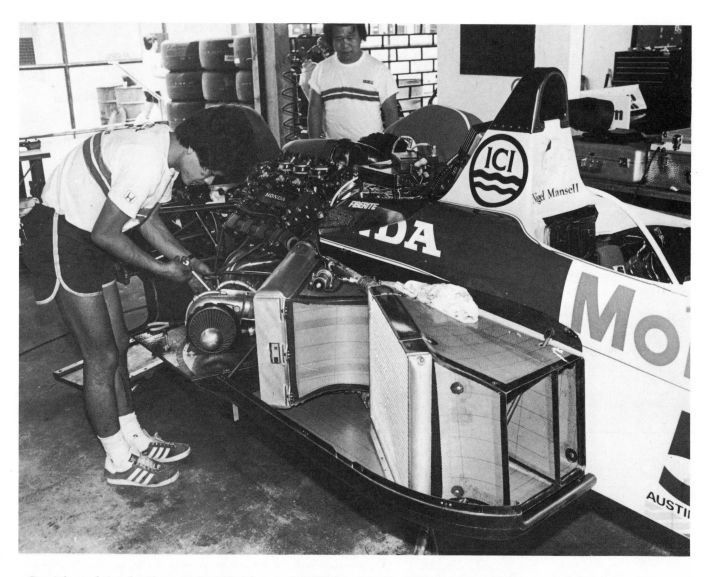

Patrick explained rather wryly: "Honda would not move the oil filter from underneath their engine despite continuous written and verbal requests from ourselves for them to do so. We were beseeching them to sit the engine 1½ in lower and put the oil filter elsewhere, which would mean we could lower the gearbox and the whole chassis as well, but Honda simply felt their engine was adequate as it was, and the best route to achieve the results they wanted was to supply it to Lotus as well . . .

"It was because of this that I decided it was not worth doing an entirely new car for 1987, which is why we did the '11B instead of a new FW12, which would have been smaller and lower, as planned. So I scrapped the FW12 . . ."

The FW11-series carbon-composite chassis lineage extends back only as far as the FW10 of 1985 – WGPE's first moulded chassis, which had replaced the aluminium-honeycomb structures to which Patrick had remained loyal for so long.

He was thus late into carbon-composite chassis structures as generally popularized by Lotus and McLaren from as early as 1981. He freely admits, "We were very slow in changing to carbon chassis. I think about that now and use it as a lesson for myself to make sure I *don't* do a similar thing again.

"However, we *could* quite happily construct a winning car out of aluminium right now – we don't have to have a carbon chassis and it's certainly not the prime reason why we didn't win as many races in 1984 as we did in 1985 and 1986.

"But I was not really too impressed by the type of failure we saw in secondary

The side pods of the FW11 were packed with radiators and turbo ancillaries.

The FW11 was lower and slimmer than its predecessor. As in the FW10, Head used a carbon/composite chassis.

components which were made in bonded composites. Things like wing support structures, wing endplates and skirts – we had seen a considerable number of them damaged. I'd also seen a considerable number of aluminium and aluminium-honeycomb chassis damaged, and the way they reacted looked a far better bet than carbon composites. I would still regard the mode of failure of aluminium structures as better than of carbon components – but we've learned an enormous amount through mandatory crash testing of nose structures, a very good thing, and without that we might not have done as many load-to-failure structure tests as we have. They have taught us a fair bit about failure of composites when overloaded. It is pretty catastrophic, so we made a nose structure designed to fail and to absorb energy

during that failure process, and we then made a chassis designed not to fail. But obviously if subjected to a big enough load it will, inevitably, fail . . .

"When Nelson crashed his car at around 160mph at Imola it went in backwards diagonally on the left-rear, after first hitting the left-front corner, which shattered the wheel and drove the upright right through the side of the forward chassis. There was a shear failure of a large area at the side of the tub there and a shear failure on top of the chassis right through both the inner and outer skins. Fortunately the floor and right-hand side had no failure, but it would not have taken much more of a load for that front part to have come right off, leaving the driver's legs exposed . . .

"The rearward impact was then absorbed by the engine and gearbox,

nothing on the tub apart from the engine mountings actually failed there. As it emerged a lot of people were patting us on the back for having built a car in which Nelson could survive a 160mph shunt, whereas in fact if he'd been unlucky and had impacted in a slight different way at a slightly different angle the story might have been very different, and a lot of people might instead have been vilifying us for building a fragile car!

"Having said that, I'm reasonably happy with the kind of structure we have now. I'm not aware of an alternative constructional method or material we could use which would give the driver a better chance in the event of an accident . . .

"Today we have the money and the people and the company size to test extensively for safety whereas in previous

years we perhaps 'hoped' we were designing for it. We design and test now for irresistible forces beyond failure. While the aerospace people do an enormous amount of fatigue testing on aircraft structures, they don't essentially load something to see whether it's strong enough. Our main criterion is rigidity. Is it *stiff* enough? And generally if it's stiff enough it's *way* strong enough.

"Today's cars are constructionally much better than before – for reasons sometimes as much concerned with making them quick as strong. High monocoque sides, concerned more with minimising the size of the holes in your tube to make it as strong as possible, contribute enormously to beam-strength and so resist any tendency for cars to break in two around the cockpit. Compare this to the low cockpit-sided

The footbox of an F1 car built after 1985 had to withstand severe impact tests. This is a 1986 FW11.

tubs like our old '07s or the Lotus 78/79 and you have to admit, yes, they were undoubtedly weak in the middle. The McLaren composite tub dating back to 1981 has been like that for years, but they compensate by adding material thickness amidships. They would undoubtedly do better to have greater cross-sectional area there . . . in my opinion.

"If one is trying to produce a monocoque chassis structure as stiff and strong as possible, one way to do it is to put the material at the outer extremities; why clothe that chassis in separate bodywork when you're using a material which can be shaped?

"But even when you've got that kind of moulded 'suppository' shape, it's wrong for people to think that because you are making it in cloth you can make it any shape you like. If you're looking for a complex shape you still have to cut and dart, and seam the cloth like a frantic tailor, and then overlap it to regain strength, and this all tends to leave you with a bad structure. Simple shapes always give better, lighter and stronger structures . . . "

Is it easy to design simply, or do designs tend to set out complicated and gain simplicity as they are refined on the drawing board?

Patrick's crisp smile broadens, "I think you tend to produce things which are simple if you're naturally lazy, because there's so much less work in drawing them. It's undoubtedly a tremendous advantage as a designer to be able to work through other designers. Some problems don't solve easily. They have to be worried and chased at. Detail is very important but you can get bogged down in the detail itself. I sometimes get great pleasure from working with somebody else using pencils on a drawing board, so that one can stand back and look at it overall and that sometimes gives you a cue to a better way of laying it out. If you do it yourself you can sometimes have your head down so long you fail to see the wood for the trees."

WGPE have an extensive CAD/CAM (Computer aided design/computer aided manufacturing) system using CALMA software and mainly Digital hardware. But Patrick "wouldn't like to comment too much on its value as a design tool because I personally don't use the CAD system. As I view it from the outside it has some very

significant advantages in helping the designer. I wouldn't say that initial inventive design is high on the list of its advantages, but we're still in the fairly early stages of using CAD to help us design our Grand Prix cars. So far we've had the system installed for 18 months; I feel we'll still be discovering some possibilities in five years time. Currently the learning curve for us is still very steep . . ."

The company was the first specialist F1 team to install its own dedicated wind tunnel facility, in 1981. It proved a vital tool in their quest for success. "As a company, we probably appreciated the significance of detailed aerodynamic study earlier than anyone except Lotus, who clearly had an initial early appreciation and then rather lost their way perhaps for detail reasons, as Peter Wright went off elsewhere or whatever. But from the middle of 1978 we realised how important aerodynamic effects are and have continued to appreciate that ever since.

"Obviously there have been times when we felt we might do things a bit better, but I don't think there's ever been a time when we thought there were aerodynamically superior cars on circuit. Aerodynamics are pretty complicated, largely because a racing car isn't a steady-state device.

"I'm not about to claim that aerodynamically we've always had the best car, but we've always been there or thereabouts, and for certain periods we have certainly led the way . . ."

With Honda turbocharged engines they have certainly done just that in 1986-87. Did the change from *c.*500bhp Cosworth power to 750bhp-plus turbo power come as a culture shock?

"Certainly turbo engines came as a different world but it didn't happen all in one go. We started off with a bit more power than a DFV or DFY and then progressively a lot more power. It was not a quantum leap. It was stepped. We had an enormous amount to learn in 1984 – as did Honda. Their programme was relatively unstructured at that time, it was virtually Kawamoto's hobby, and it didn't really become properly structured with proper project management systems until mid '85. The biggest problem was simply that the engine was diabolically unreliable.

"This can be due to both installation problems and inherent problems within the engine. In that particular case I would

left
The new FW11's bodywork was designed on the freshly installed CAD/CAM system.

A familiar sight in 1987: the Williams of Piquet and Mansell dominating from the front of the grid, as here at Jerez. Mansell bustled past Piquet on the opening lap, was never headed and seemed on course for the title. Another win in Mexico, with Piquet second, underlined this but then came that heavy crash during qualifying at Suzuka which ruled him out of the remaining two races.

below
The Williams FW11.

Piquet in second place holding off Gerhard Berger in a Ferrari in the 1987 French Grand Prix at Paul Ricard.

At Monaco in 1985 Mansell practised second fastest to Alain Prost having outqualified his then team mate Keke Rosberg. Brake problems intervened during the race and he had to be content with seventh place.

In three seasons at Williams, Nigel Mansell improved dramatically. His record at the end of 1987 was 13 wins from a total of 46 races.

Complex plumbing of a Honda turbo installation. Overleaf is a similar view with the hydraulic system for active suspension added.

say it was 80 per cent in the engine and 20 per cent in the installation. But like all problems they have solutions, and there was no structure which could identify the problems before looking at the solutions. That structure at Honda was not set up until late '84 and it didn't start having an effect until mid '85.

"Honda kept us pretty well in the picture through 1985-86, but became more secretive early in '87 and by the middle and end of the season had become very secretive indeed . . . We had a very good working relationship with many of their junior engineers, the chaps who worked closely with us, but higher management levels were often . . . inscrutable . . ."

Looking towards 3.5-litre naturally-aspirated racing in 1988 with the new Judd V8: "While I have to admit I really find the turbo engine more interesting than a naturally-aspirated one, for many reasons, I do ask myself what will I think in a year's time? Will I then prefer natur-

ally- aspirated engines, and will we have found more potential in them than seems to be the case at the moment?

"I most certainly look forward to renewing our association with John Judd. In 1981 we ran Judd rebuilt and prepared DFVs and in '82-'83 Judd-Williams modified DFVs. We won the Championship together in '82 – albeit due to Ferrari crashes and Renault confusing themselves, but that was all with John Judd. Working with him was a great pleasure because he doesn't build a wall of secrecy around his company on the basis that if 'they' don't know what goes on then 'they' won't realise how little we know.

"John is very open, certainly he has been with us, and to be aware again of what is happening on the engine side will be very interesting . . . I think that contrary to what some sections of the media might think, we've still got a future in Formula 1 . . ."

Williams Active Ride

by Doug Nye

Williams Grand Prix Engineering and, coincidentally, Team Lotus, started writing a new chapter in motor racing history in 1987, by not just contesting, but actually winning races with computer-controlled hydraulic suspension cars.

Williams logged hundreds of test miles with their active machine before winning first-time-out in Italy. That was the beginning of a three-race programme which ended in Spain with a placing tally that made sweet music in designer Frank Dernie's ears – first, third and fourth.

Back in the 1950s, BRM toyed with a Citroën-style gas-filled suspension system for Formula 1. More recently Ligier ran a broadly similar system, and for road cars Automotive Products have toyed rather half-heartedly with an active suspension related distantly to Citroën's ride-levelling systems. Williams Grand Prix Engineering began co-development of this AP active-ride system in 1985, investigating possible adaptation to Formula 1, mainly – it would appear – to maintain an optimum ride attitude for maximum aerodynamic advantage.

Engineer Bob Pitcher had headed AP's active group and Williams co-operated with him for a couple of years, before AP opted out, leaving the co-developers to go their separate ways; Pitcher continued in his own right – I understand largely for off-road and agricultural vehicles – while the Williams R & D group under Frank Dernie set about redesigning both the basic system and the way it worked.

The team started running the system in its current form in December 1986 – and even after Piquet's debut win at Monza, chief engineer Patrick Head said: "We have still got an awful lot of work to do . . . One way of looking at it is that ideally we should begin racing promising R & D projects at the beginning of a year, not at the end. The positive way of looking at it says that we've started early for next season . . . "

Nelson Piquet gave the active ride Williams a debut victory at Monza, but as there was still a lot more work to be done on the system it was not taken to late-season races outside Europe.

The hydraulic pump can be seen on the FW11B virtually dead centre between the rear wheels.

The Williams-Honda FW11B "Active-ride" cars used a lightweight hydraulic pressure pump driven off the camshaft tail to maintain pressure within an accumulator. Each suspension corner has a strut and gas spring mounted in series to handle all high-frequency bumps and ripples, interacting with a valve allowing hydraulic fluid in and out of the strut under pressure to control its mean length. A rheostat connected to each strut signals changes in its length to the control computer, which can be programmed to trigger suitable responses from hydraulic valve blocks feeding the gas-spring spheres, in which pressurised fluid is separated from the gas by flexible diaphragms.

"We are not setting out to control the car as it goes over a bump, but on the back side of the bump the spring rebounds to maintain ride level. The system also handles anti-roll control, and with four struts and a control system we are trying to exercise a degree of control over the plane of the car, independent of what load is acting upon it. We are attempting to maintain an attitude."

Patrick was typically wary of making loud claims for this system, beyond a cautious "drivers seem able to maintain very consistent lap times with it". The first question down-to-earth Williams engineers asked was simply "Are we going quicker?", not "Are the drivers feeling more comfortable?" – although their car can of course be set up that way, and one can affect the other.

Patrick is tired of being asked if the Williams system is 'simpler' than Lotus', purely because ". . . this pre-supposes we fully understand the Lotus system, which we do not". His system does, however, have fewer sensors around the car and is less compromised by any background of development essentially for road cars. In other words Lotus Active may be immensely over-capable for Formula 1, while the apparently less expensive Williams system is more finely-targeted, and perhaps capable enough. Obviously it also involves a weight penalty, but its power consumption is very small – less than 5 bhp – and presupposing that Williams have answered the question "Can we get quick-enough response?" they are now apparently working hard on "Can we get it working properly again and again?"

Williams Drivers

by Alan Henry

Alan Jones

"The great thing about Alan, apart from his enormous determination, was his ability to lift the team's morale when things were going badly. In that respect, he was something of an inspiration to the mechanics. And I don't believe that many drivers have that particularly quality."

That is Patrick Head's assessment of Alan Jones as a person, as a team member. His contribution to the team's fortunes as a driver are legend. Talk to the Williams personnel and you still get the feeling that 'Jonesey' was a bit special, different to all the others, even seven years after he won the team's first World Championship. Some people believe that Frank and Patrick have never enjoyed such a close working relationship with a driver from that day to this . . .

Jones and Williams were thrown together when nobody else seemed to want either of them. The rugged son of Stan Jones, one of Austalian motor racing's favourite, hard driving, hard

Alan Jones.

drinking postwar heroes, Alan flirted with F1 as a member of the Hill and Surtees teams in 1975 and 1976. But when Tom Pryce was killed at Kyalami in 1977, he was drafted into the Shadow team as a replacement for the Welshman and turned a few heads by winning the Austrian Grand Prix in a car that had little business being at the sharp end of the field.

That success put Jones in the public eye and, as Frank Williams set about rebuilding his Grand Prix challenge in 1978, Alan stood out as the obvious man for the job. Armed with Patrick's ultra-compact FW06, Jones got in amongst the Ferraris battling for the lead at Long Beach. That was the day Frank realised he had found himself an extra special driver.

Second place in the United States GP at Watkins Glen was proof that the partnership was on a winning trail, and when Head's superb ground-effects FW07 came in the following year, Jones squeezed every ounce of potential out of it. Although his team-mate Clay Regazzoni won Williams' first Grand Prix at Silverstone after Jones retired, Alan triumphed at Hockenheim, Oster-reichring, Zandvoort and Montreal.

The following season, Alan sustained his winning momentum to take the Championship title with wins in Buenos Aires, Jarama (non-championship), Paul Ricard, Brands Hatch, Montreal and Watkins Glen. He would have retained his title in 1981 but for a trifling series of technical problems; as it was he continued to drive superbly and rounded off the season with a splendid flag-to-flag triumph in the inaugural Las Vegas Grand Prix. Then he quit the cockpit and retired to his native Australia, despite all Williams' efforts to make him change his mind.

But Alan had retired too early and soon got itchy feet. He returned to the cockpit briefly in 1983 for Arrows, then did a full season for the Haas Lola team in 1986. But the machinery was not top class and there was to be no magical recapture of that blindingly quick, overwhelmingly confident and committed form which was his hallmark in his heyday at Williams.

One can only speculate as to what Jones might have achieved had he stayed with Frank through the Williams-Honda era. The combination would have been worth watching. No question about it.

Carlos Reutemann

Carlos came to Williams fresh from a disappointing single-year stay at Lotus in 1979, but his two and a bit seasons with Frank's team never saw him quite realise the potential his obvious talent always signalled. In many ways, his recruitment to the team was typical of Frank's tendency, whether deliberate or inadvertent, to set his drivers at each other's throats.

Alan Jones had been comfortable with Clay Regazzoni as his number two in 1979. Clay was quick enough to get the job done when Jones' car faltered – as he proved at Silverstone – and was content with his role as number two. Reutemann was nominally number two, but the dour Argentinian was in truth too good a driver for such secondary status to rest easily on his shoulders.

In 1980 he won a single Grand Prix, at Monaco, after Jones and Didier Pironi's Ligier dropped out ahead of him. But in 1981 he clearly felt the time was ripe for a World Championship challenge. He kicked off the season by winning the Brazilian Grand Prix at Rio against team orders, opting to ignore specific pit signals instructing him to fall back behind Jones. He didn't, and the team imposed a financial penalty on him as a result. Of course, Alan was fit to be tied . . .

Reutemann in the FW07C.

A succession of good performances throughout the year brought Reutemann to the threshold of the World Championship as the teams arrived in Las Vegas for the second (and last) race round the Caesar's Palace car park. A stupendous qualifying lap earned him a commanding pole position, but in the race he just capitulated. He faded to eighth at the chequered flag, handing the title to Nelson Piquet. There were a few mumbled excuses about the car not handling quite right, but no real explanation. It was almost as if he did not really want to be World Champion.

After two races of the 1982 season, he retired from the cockpit. It was a spontaneous decision which he never went back on. Now he will freely admit that he quit too soon. A genuine and charming man, Carlos Reutemann none the less remains something of an enigmatic character in the Grand Prix history books. He never quite managed to get it all together.

left
Carlos Reutemann.

Keke Rosberg

"Somehow, you know, I think the Williams team never quite forgave me for not being Alan Jones . . ." A typically glib remark from F1's King of the throwaway lines, yet strangely true in some ways. Keke Rosberg came marching into the Williams camp as everybody was still commiserating with each other over Jones' retirement. And, truth be told, none of them quite knew what to make of this chain-smoking Finn whose off-track behaviour was highlighted by a level of candour regarded as outrageous by some members of the team.

Keke got his break at a late-1981 Paul Ricard test session. Neither Frank Williams nor Patrick Head were present, so it was largely down to Frank Dernie and Charlie Crichton-Stuart to make an assessment of this cocky Finn whose F1 form to date, with Theodore and Wolf/ Fittipaldi, could hardly be described as significant. Armed with Patrick's new

FW08, the newcomer barnstormed his spectacular way to the 1982 World Championship.

He only won a single race – the Swiss GP at Dijon – but drove superbly for most of the year. The biggest disappointment was a splendid pole for the British GP at Brands Hatch – and a back row start after fuel vapourisation prevented him getting away as scheduled at the start of the parade lap. In 1983 he won Monaco, in the now flat-bottomed FW08C on a slippery track, and produced probably the best win of his career at Dallas in 1984 to give the Williams-Honda alliance the first of 23 victories.

Keke stayed on at Williams until the end of 1985, winning two more races (Detroit and Adelaide) for the team, and then moved on for a final year's racing with McLaren before retiring from the cockpit. Outspokenly opposed to the signing of Nigel Mansell at the start of 1985, Rosberg pleaded with Williams to be released from his 1985 contract because he reckoned "Mansell meant trouble." But Keke was honest enough to change his opinions and admit he was wrong; by the summer of 1985 he was getting on with Nigel like a house on fire. However, he didn't change his mind about transferring to McLaren.

At the height of his achievement, Keke's opposite-lock, hard driving style used to drive Patrick Head round the bend. The Williams designer could often be found muttering, "Why can't he understand that he would be even quicker if he tidied up his style?"

It made no difference to Keke. "I like driving this way – and until somebody can prove to me that it's the wrong way, that's the way I'll continue," he said firmly. Nothing could be more typical of the popular Rosberg than a remark like that!

Derek Daly

A genial Irishman with the gift of the gab, 'DD' was signed up to partner Rosberg after Reutemann's sudden retirement from the scene two races into the '82 Grand Prix season. Derek had perviously raced for Tyrrell and RAM March in F1 and there were signs that his career was running out of steam slightly when he was snatched up to run alongside Keke in 1982.

Derek Daly.

He was quick enough in pure racing terms, but Williams reckoned he was not a good enough qualifier. Too much of his time was spent battling into contention from lowly grid positions, they said. Daly responded by itemising the problems he had suffered during practice at each individual race . . .

Daly ran well on several occasions, almost winning the bizarre Monaco Grand Prix where everybody either crashed or ran out of fuel. He had wiped off his FW08C's rear wing when he spun into a guard rail, but suddenly rocketed

Daly's single season with Williams v. as punctuated by alarming incidents. Here a wheel nut has parted company during qualifying at Hockenheim. Daly ended the year with eight points in the Driver's Championship, which did not reflect his true ability.

into contention a few laps from the finish as many faster runners slowed, out of fuel. But that spin had also knocked off the gearbox oil cooler and the Williams rolled to a halt with seized transmission a couple of corners from home. It was the closest he ever came to a Grand Prix win because he was dropped from the team at the end of the season.

Jacques Laffite

At the height of the acrimonious FOCA/FISA wars in 1981, Frank Williams made it clear that he would "never sign a French driver". Presumably good old Jacques was an honorary Brit, because Frank signed him up at the end of 1982 and he stayed on the team strength for two seasons before being succeeded by Nigel Mansell.

Jacques, of course, is a highly respected Williams Old Boy. Back in the dark days of 1974, when Frank was running his Iso-Marlboros on a financial shoestring, sometimes making his business calls from a phone box close to Reading speedway track, Laffite saved the team's financial bacon. He nursed Frank's old crate to second place in the German Grand Prix at Nürburgring. It put money in the bank at a crucial moment.

In 1976 Jacques went off to Ligier and stayed there for seven years. Then he came back and joined Williams. It is fair to comment that his talent had peaked by then but, as Keke Rosberg always reminded us, "Jacques is as good as his car".

So it proved. In 1983, driving the FW08C, he shared the second row of the grid at Long Beach with Keke – and he ran second in the Finn's wheeltracks at Monaco until the gearbox broke. But in 1984, driving the unloved FW09-Honda, Jacques took a more relaxed view of things. It wasn't a winner, so what the hell . . .

So he went back to Ligier for 1985 – and got a lot of pleasure from running ahead of Mansell's Williams at the Nürburgring. Infectiously enthusiastic, disarmingly straightforward and universally popular, they still love him at Didcot to this day.

top right
Nigel Mansell surrounded by admiring fans.

bottom right
Mansell burns rubber to delight the grandstand crowd at the Tribute to Williams Day, Brands Hatch, 1986.

left
Jacques Laffite.

Nigel Mansell

Signed up as number two to Keke Rosberg, Mansell developed into England's top contemporary Grand Prix driver thanks largely to the sympathetic handling he received at Williams from the start of 1985. It was, in his view, a far cry from the diet of hostility which had been rammed down his throat by Peter Warr at Team Lotus.

Not that Nigel's maiden season with Frank's team was without its hiccups. He spun off on the very first corner of the very first race in Brazil, and survived a 200mph shunt at Paul Ricard during practice for the French Grand Prix. There still seemed to be an erratic streak to his driving, but he nailed it, seemingly once and for all, with brilliant wins in the Grand Prix of Europe at Brands Hatch and the South African Grand Prix at Kyalami at the end of the year.

Then came 1986 and 1987, and the two spectacular challenges for the World Championship. Eclipsing newly signed team leader Nelson Piquet on many occasions in 1986, Mansell barnstormed to victory in Belgium, Canada, France, Britain and Portugal before losing his chance of the title in the most famous tyre explosion of all time, at Adelaide in the last race of the season. But he had done more than sufficient to earn his Formula 1 spurs.

The 1987 season brought more of the same. Nigel's driving style seemed to be even less inhibited than it had been through the previous summer. Consistently eclipsing Piquet for sheer speed, he hurtled to victories at Imola, Paul Ricard, Silverstone, Osterreichring, Jerez and Mexico. It was all flat-out, teetering-on-the-limit stuff. Yet still that impetuous streak emerged from time to time. He took Senna off on the first lap at Spa, then wrote himself out of the title chase with a huge accident at Suzuka, practising for the Japanese Grand Prix.

As Patrick Head says, there is absolutely nothing about Mansell's performance in the cockpit of a racing car which suggests he is anything but a naturally gifted racing driver. Out of the cockpit, Nigel is a less complete performer. He still displays that streak of the underdog, believing that the world is against him. And he will seldom concede that he is wrong . . .

Nelson Piquet

Thrice World Champion, winner of 20 Grands Prix, yet one of the most controversial and difficult to assess drivers of the past few years. That's Nelson Piquet, the man Frank Williams signed for the 'big buck' in 1986 – and who failed to match up to Mansell in lap-for-lap racing situations for virtually his entire two year career driving for Frank's team.

It is now clear that there was a major misunderstanding when Piquet signed his two year contract as number one driver. Nelson thought he was going to receive preferential treatment, to the extent that the team's number two driver would be obliged to follow along behind in a genuine supporting role. Frank and the team's management saw Nelson's number one status in terms of the equipment and support he would be given. In their view, out on the circuits it would be down to him.

He kicked off 1986 with a win at Rio, leaving Mansell in the wall after a first-lap collision with Senna's Lotus. On the strength of that showing, Nelson could be forgiven for feeling over-confident. But he didn't win again until Hockenheim, and although more successes followed at Budapest and Monza, the championship

slipped from his grasp at Adelaide as it did for Mansell.

In 1987 Piquet found no change to the team's operational format. Badly shaken up in a violent Imola practice accident, Nelson continued to rail at his treatment. In his view he did not get number one status. "I didn't come here as number one, being paid a lot of money, to race my team mate," he would fume. But that's the position he found himself in. He didn't like it, so he opted for a move to Lotus for 1988. There he would have what he liked best – effectively a one car team with all the attention focussed on him.

If your index of a driver's status is results on paper, then Nelson Piquet ranks amongst the great ones. His position on that pedestal becomes rather more precarious if you put a premium on the *way* in which a racing driver achieves his results.

The stand-ins . . .

Two drivers who raced for Williams on a one-off basis between 1980 and 1987 were Mario Andretti and Riccardo Patrese. Mario drove in the 1982 Long Beach race, retiring early after a brush with the wall, while Patrese deputised for the injured Mansell in Adelaide at the end of 1987, retiring with engine trouble. They were inconclusive outings by drivers whose quality had been proven in different machinery.

Chassis by Chassis

by Bruce Jones

Pescarolo rounds Druids hairpin at Brands Hatch in the Politoys FX3's solitary Grand Prix.

POLITOYS FX3 Penned by Len Bailey, the FX3 was the first Williams, although named 'Politoys' after its sponsor, and used the ubiquitous 2993cc Ford Cosworth DFV V8. The car had but one 1972 Grand Prix outing, at the British GP at Brands Hatch, lasting only seven laps before a fiery accident. **Driver:** Henri Pescarolo.

FX3B Updated FX3s for the start of the 1973 season, running in the colours of Marlboro and entitled 'Iso Marlboro', used until Iso's first eponymous car could be introduced. Grid-fillers rather than mid-fielders. **Drivers:** Howden Ganley, Nanni Galli, Jackie Pretorius.

IR01-IR04/FW01-FW03 Designed by John Clarke. Again Cosworth DFV-powered, the 1974 car was developed without much success as Williams had to run a series of rent-a-drive men. Iso-Rivolta, as makers of high-performance Italian cars, can have gained little prestige from this association. **Drivers:** Gijs van Lennep, Jacky Ickx, Howden Ganley, Nanni Galli, Henri Pescarolo, Graham McRae, Tim Schenken, Arturo Merzario, Tom Belso, Jacques Laffite, Tony Brise, Damien Magee, Jo Vonlanthen, Renzo Zorzi, Ian Scheckter.

FW04 Designed for 1975 as a continuation of the IR/FW range. Unlike the earlier models, it had a full-width nose section, and it also achieved some success, with Jacques Laffite scoring a second place in the German GP – the team's only points of the year. **Drivers:** Jacques Laffite, Arturo Merzario, Renzo Zorzi.

FW05 Conceived as the Hesketh 308C. Cosworth engine. Williams took over the Harvey Postlethwaite design when the Hesketh team folded. Backed by Austro-Canadian millionaire, Walter Wolf, for his 1976 programme. **Drivers:** Jacky Ickx, Michel Leclare, Arturo Merzario, Hans Binder, Warwick Brown.

FW06 After a season running a March-Cosworth for Patrick Neve in 1977, Williams returned with its own design for 1978. Patrick Head had the lightweight car ready for the first GP. Competitive from the beginning, the simple and compact design carried Williams to the forefront of the sport. Financed by money from the Arab world. **Drivers:** Alan Jones, Clay Regazzoni.

FW07 The first ground-effects Williams, again designed by Patrick Head. Introduced in time for the start of the European season in 1979 and immediately on the pace. Victorious in its fifth race, the British GP, driven by Clay Regazzoni; this was the first GP win by a Williams. The FW07 was then proved to be the most effective gound-effects Cosworth chassis of the period as Alan Jones won four of the next five GPs. **Drivers:** Alan Jones, Clay Regazzoni, Rupert Keegan.

FW07C The change to C-specification was made during the winter of 1980, a slimmer monocoque being adopted along with revised bodywork, variable-rate springing and a wider front track. The change to the springing was unsuccessful and was dropped immediately, for these were the infamous days of hydraulic suspension set-ups that were used to keep cars from scraping the road when in the pit road, yet yield to aerodynamic pressure at speed so as to achieve the ground effects required. **Drivers:** Alan Jones, Carlos Reutemann, Keke Rosberg, Mario Andretti.

Clay Regazzoni had the distinction of providing Williams with their first GP success in the FW07.

Alan Jones and the FW06
were immediately
competitive.

below
The FW07C shows the
basic layout of a late-
1970s F1 car, with the
driver well forward in a
narrow monocoque, a
single fuel cell behind him
and then the relatively
small DFV engine.

FW08 Described by Head as a " tidied up, stiffened version of the FW07 – the front suspension is new, but the rear is like the old car." Remained with aluminium honeycomb construction rather than following fashion for carbon/Kevlar. Sufficiently efficient for Rosberg to land the 1982 World title with one win. **Drivers:** Keke Rosberg, Derek Daly.

FW08C For 1983, the most visible modification was shorter sidepods, with the radiators mounted further back. The rear suspension was new, but otherwise it was very little different from the FW08. Rosberg put it on pole on its debut, ahead of all the more powerful turbo cars. The venerable Cosworth DFV was soon outgunned, though. **Drivers:** Keke Rosberg, Jacques Laffite, Jonathan Palmer.

FW09 1.5 litre Given its debut at the South African GP at the end of 1983 using the Honda V6 turbocharged engine. It finished fifth, which augured well. Box-like and extremely ugly, with long sidepods again, the FW09 at least had the power to counter its turbocharged rivals and so did not require the handling advantage upon which the normally aspirated cars relied. The main problem was harnessing the extra horsepower. This car was a disappointment, marred by understeer. **Drivers:** Keke Rosberg, Jacques Laffite.

Reigning World Champion Keke Rosberg in an FW08C.

right
Jacques Laffite did not enjoy the same fortune as Rosberg when he raced an FW09-Honda for the first time at Kyalami.

below
Derek Daly scrambled home fifth in an FW08 after a mighty tussle with de Angelis and Prost during the 1982 British Grand Prix at Brands Hatch.

The FW09B, unloved by Rosberg and Laffite. Rear winglets were later banned.

Rosberg in an FW10.

Mansell in an FW11,
which won Williams the
Constructors title.

Piquet won the World
Championship in the
FW11B.

FW09B Introduced midway through the 1984 season. Wheelbase altered in an attempt to cure understeer, but as unloved as its predecessor. **Drivers:** Keke Rosberg, Jacques Laffite.

FW10 Patrick Head made amends for the FW09 with this the first carbonfibre composite Williams, designed and built in-house. Repositioned radiator, exhaust and turbo layout to improve airflow. Body profile very much in the 'Coke bottle' shape prevalent in the mid-eighties but still boxy. Money no longer coming from Saudia, but primarily from Canon, Mobil, ICI and Denim. This was the car that put the Williams-Honda partnership into the limelight, rounding out the season with three wins from the last three races. **Drivers:** Keke Rosberg, Nigel Mansell.

FW11 New design ready for the start of the 1986 season, driven to win first time out by Nelson Piquet. Slightly narrower and lower than the FW10. Made to accommodate drop to 195-litre fuel allowance. CAD/CAM-designed body, with revised suspension. Williams still enjoyed Honda power exclusivity with F-type V6, and absolutely dominated the Constructors championship, yet somehow neither driver contrived to land the Drivers' crown. Nine GP wins in the one season. **Drivers:** Nigel Mansell, Nelson Piquet.

FW11B For 1987, Honda power was no longer for Williams only. Chassis updated to B spec, which meant using Frank Dernie designed, computer controlled hydraulic 'active' suspension. Piquet did most of the development, Mansell having "had his fill" of such suspension at Lotus. FW11B then did not use 'active' suspension until later in the season. That aside, there was very little change over the FW11. **Drivers:** Nigel Mansell, Nelson Piquet, Riccardo Patrese.

GRAND PRIX VICTORIES

	Year	Event	Chassis-Engine	Driver (Nat)
1	1979	British GP – Silverstone	Williams-Cosworth FW07	Clay Regazzoni (CH)
2		German GP – Hockenheim	Williams-Cosworth FW07	Alan Jones (AUS)
3		Austrian GP – Österreichring	Williams-Cosworth FW07	Alan Jones (AUS)
4		Dutch GP – Zandvoort	Williams-Cosworth FW07	Alan Jones (AUS)
5		Canadian GP – Montreal	Williams-Cosworth FW07	Alan Jones (AUS)
6	1980	Argentine GP – Buenos Aires	Williams-Cosworth FW07	Alan Jones (AUS)
7		Monaco GP	Williams-Cosworth FW07B	Carlos Reutemann (RA)
8		French GP – Paul Ricard	Williams-Cosworth FW07B	Alan Jones (AUS)
9		British GP – Brand's Hatch	Williams-Cosworth FW07B	Alan Jones (AUS)
10		Canadian GP – Montreal	Williams-Cosworth FW07B	Alan Jones (AUS)
11		US GP East – Watkins Glen	Williams-Cosworth FW07B	Alan Jones (AUS)
12	1981	US GP West – Long Beach	Williams-Cosworth FW07C	Alan Jones (AUS)
13		Brazilian GP – Jacarepagua	Williams-Cosworth FW07C	Carlos Reutemann (RA)
14		Belgian GP – Zolder	Williams-Cosworth FW07C	Carlos Reutemann (RA)
15		Las Vegas GP	Williams-Cosworth FW07C	Alan Jones (AUS)
16	1982	Swiss GP – Dijon	Williams-Cosworth FW08	Keke Rosberg (SF)
17	1983	Monaco GP	Williams-Cosworth FW08C	Keke Rosberg (SF)
18	1985	US GP – Dallas	Williams-Honda FW09	Keke Rosberg (SF)
19	1985	US GP – Detroit	Williams-Honda FW010	Keke Rosberg (SF)
20		European GP – Brands Hatch	Williams-Honda FW10B	Nigel Mansell (GB)
21		South Africa GP – Kyalami	Williams-Honda FW10B	Nigel Mansell (GB)
22		Australian GP – Adelaide	Williams-Honda FW10B	Keke Rosberg (SF)
23	1986	Brazilian GP – Jacarepagua	Williams-Honda FW11	Nelson Piquet (BR)
24		Belgian GP – Spa-Francorchamps	Williams-Honda FW11	Nigel Mansell (GB)
25		Canadian GP – Montreal	Williams-Honda FW11	Nigel Mansell (GB)
26		French GP – Paul Ricard	Williams-Honda FW11	Nigel Mansell (GB)
27		British GP – Brands Hatch	Williams-Honda FW11	Nigel Mansell (GB)
28		German GP – Hockenheim	Williams-Honda FW11	Nelson Piquet (BR)
29		Hungarian GP – Hungaroring	Williams-Honda FW11	Nelson Piquet (BR)
30		Italian GP – Monza	Williams-Honda FW11	Nelson Piquet (BR)
31		Portuguese GP – Estoril	Williams-Honda FW11	Nigel Mansell (GB)
32	1987	San Marino GP – Imola	Williams-Honda FW11B	Nigel Mansell (GB)
33		French GP – Paul Ricard	Williams-Honda FW11B	Nigel Mansell (GB)
34		British GP – Silverstone	Williams-Honda FW11B	Nigel Mansell (GB)
35		German GP – Hockenheim	Williams-Honda FW11B	Nelson Piquet (BR)
36		Hungarian GP – Hungaroring	Williams-Honda FW11B	Nelson Piquet (BR)
37		Austrian GP – Österreichring	Williams-Honda FW11B	Nigel Mansell (GB)
38		Italian GP – Monza	Williams-Honda FW11B	Nelson Piquet (BR)
39		Spanish GP – Jerez	Williams-Honda FW11B	Nigel Mansell (GB)
40		Mexican GP – Mexico City	Williams-Honda FW11B	Nigel Mansell (GB)

AUTOSPORT

THE WORLD'S LEADING MOTOR SPORT WEEKLY

In the motor racing world, AUTOSPORT magazine is indispensable.

Its weekly look at the motor racing scene is regarded by enthusiasts and those involved in the sport as the primary source of news and factual information.

A status it has held almost from the day it was launched in 1950.

Every week its pages are packed with authoritative news items, event reports and features.

Its colour coverage of the glamorous and fast action world of big league motorsport, epitomised by Formula One Grand Prix and World Championship Rallying, is unbeatable.

Every major motor sport event in the world is covered. Every important result is covered, no matter where it's happened.

In fact, practically everything that goes on in motor racing finds its way onto the pages of AUTOSPORT.

And all within days of happening.

EVERY THURSDAY